Battle Orders • 31

The Royal Navy 1793–1815

Gregory Fremont-Barnes

Consultant Editor Dr Duncan Anderson • *Series editors* Marcus Cowper and Nikolai Bogdanovic

First published in Great Britain in 2007 by Osprey Publishing,
Midland House, West Way, Botley, Oxford OX2 0PH, UK
443 Park Avenue South, New York, NY 10016, USA
E-mail: info@ospreypublishing.com

A CIP catalogue record for this book is available from the British Library

ISBN: 978 1 84603 138 0

Editorial by Ilios Publishing Ltd, Oxford, UK (www.iliospublishing.com)
Page layout by Bounford.com, Huntingdon, UK
Index by ALan Thatcher
Typeset in GillSans and Stone Serif
Originated by United Graphics, Singapore
Printed in China through Bookbuilders

07 08 09 10 11   10 9 8 7 6 5 4 3 2 1

FOR A CATALOGUE OF ALL BOOKS PUBLISHED BY OSPREY MILITARY AND
AVIATION PLEASE CONTACT:

NORTH AMERICA
Osprey Direct, c/o Random House Distribution Center, 400 Hahn Road,
Westminster, MD 21157, USA
E-mail: info@ospreydirect.com

ALL OTHER REGIONS
Osprey Direct UK, PO Box 140 Wellingborough, Northants, NN8 2FA, UK
E-mail: info@ospreydirect.co.uk

www.ospreypublishing.com

Contents

Introduction

During the French Revolutionary and Napoleonic Wars, fought over the course of two decades between 1793 and 1815, the Royal Navy established its reputation as one of the most effective fighting institutions in history. The Navy's primary objective was to achieve and maintain naval dominance – that is to say, control of the sea – an aim secured as a consequence of its superiority in leadership, morale, seamanship and gunnery. Not only did the Navy play a fundamental part in the defeat of France, it periodically opposed, usually with remarkable success, her allies, Holland, Spain and Denmark, so establishing a maritime supremacy which would remain unchallenged for the next hundred years.

Nelson boarding the *San Josef* at the battle of St Vincent, 14 February 1797. Acting without orders, Nelson boldly left the line and placed his 74, the *Captain* in the path of a group of Spanish ships seeking to flee from the action, in so doing colliding with the *San Nicolas* (84), which in turn crashed into the *San Josef* (112). Nelson immediately boarded the former and, discovering the captain had surrendered, crossed onto the deck of the *San Josef*, thus capturing two enemy ships in succession – a feat later described as 'Nelson's Patent Bridge for Boarding First Rates'. (Umhey Collection)

Number of first to sixth rate ships at key points, 1793–1815			
1 Jan	Type	Number	Tonnage
1793	Line	26	44,116
	Total	83	87,893
1803	Line	32	54,800
	Total	116	131,367
1805	Line	83	148,929
	Total	209	261,491
1815	Line	47	85,804
	Total	188	213,472

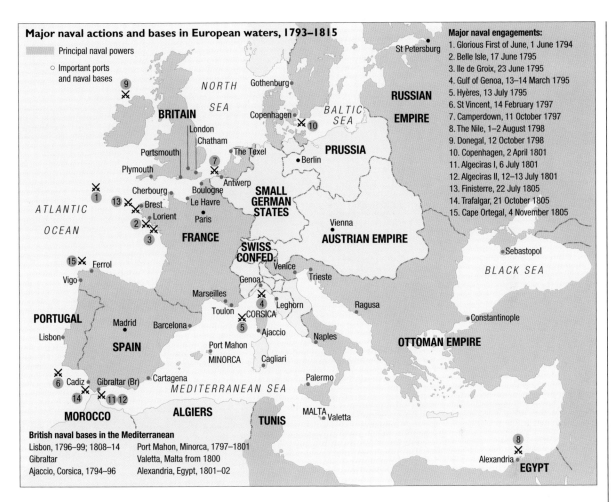

Major naval actions and bases in European waters, 1793–1815

Principal naval powers

○ Important ports and naval bases

NORTH SEA
ATLANTIC OCEAN
BALTIC SEA
BLACK SEA
MEDITERRANEAN SEA

RUSSIAN EMPIRE
St Petersburg
Sebastopol

BRITAIN
London
Chatham
Portsmouth
Plymouth
Gothenburg
Copenhagen

PRUSSIA
Berlin

SMALL GERMAN STATES

AUSTRIAN EMPIRE
Vienna

SWISS CONFED.

The Texel
Antwerp
Boulogne
Le Havre
Cherbourg
Brest
Lorient
Paris

FRANCE

Venice
Trieste
Ragusa
Genoa
Marseilles
Toulon
Leghorn
CORSICA
Ajaccio

Ferrol
Vigo

PORTUGAL
Lisbon

SPAIN
Madrid
Barcelona
Cartagena
Port Mahon
MINORCA
Cagliari

Naples
Palermo

Constantinople

OTTOMAN EMPIRE

Cadiz
Gibraltar (Br)

MOROCCO
ALGIERS
TUNIS
MALTA Valetta

Alexandria
EGYPT

Major naval engagements:
1. Glorious First of June, 1 June 1794
2. Belle Isle, 17 June 1795
3. Ile de Groix, 23 June 1795
4. Gulf of Genoa, 13–14 March 1795
5. Hyères, 13 July 1795
6. St Vincent, 14 February 1797
7. Camperdown, 11 October 1797
8. The Nile, 1–2 August 1798
9. Donegal, 12 October 1798
10. Copenhagen, 2 April 1801
11. Algeciras I, 6 July 1801
12. Algeciras II, 12–13 July 1801
13. Finisterre, 22 July 1805
14. Trafalgar, 21 October 1805
15. Cape Ortegal, 4 November 1805

British naval bases in the Mediterranean
Lisbon, 1796–99; 1808–14
Gibraltar
Ajaccio, Corsica, 1794–96
Port Mahon, Minorca, 1797–1801
Valetta, Malta from 1800
Alexandria, Egypt, 1801–02

Such was the superiority of the Royal Navy that it emerged victorious in every major encounter at sea during the French Revolutionary and Napoleonic Wars. A good deal of its other roles, however, are not so easily represented by cartography, including blockade duty, the war on commerce, amphibious operations, coastal patrolling and raids, and the protection of merchantmen in convoys.

The *Indefatigable* (44) and *Amazon* (36) take on the larger, though damaged, *Droits de l'Homme* (74), off the French coast on 13–14 January 1797. Having fled from an abortive expedition to Bantry Bay on the Irish coast, the French third rate encountered the two British frigates, both on blockade duty off Brest. (Stratford Archive)

List of active ships, 1793–1802 – the French Revolutionary Wars

Class	1793	1794	1795	1796	1797	1798	1799	1800	1801	1802
First rates	5	6	6	6	6	6	6	6	6	6
Second rates	16	16	17	16	16	17	17	16	16	16
Third rates	92	95	91	94	94	97	102	101	105	104
Total of the line	**113**	**117**	**114**	**116**	**116**	**120**	**125**	**123**	**127**	**126**
Fourth rates	12	12	12	21	16	16	14	14	13	13
Fifth rates	79	84	102	106	115	123	117	112	113	120
Sixth rates	35	36	35	37	40	41	42	34	34	28
Sloops	40	53	62	84	91	94	98	107	104	98
Bombs	2	2	2	2	2	11	15	15	14	14
Fireships	5	3	3	3	3	3	7	7	3	2
Brigs, cutters, etc.	18	21	33	36	52	94	99	97	103	104
Grand total	**304**	**328**	**363**	**405**	**435**	**502**	**517**	**509**	**511**	**505**

Operating throughout the oceans of the world, from the Channel, the North and Baltic Seas, to the Atlantic, the Mediterranean, the West Indies and beyond, the Navy defended Britain's trade routes and contributed to the expansion and defence of her empire; prevented the enemy from making use of its colonial resources and raw materials; made possible the dispatch of expeditionary forces (as well as fleets) wherever Britain chose, especially to seize enemy colonies; and enabled Britain to protect and pursue her own interests, and those of her allies. Above all, the Navy provided the nation's first line of defence against invasion.

This study examines the structure of the Royal Navy – the government apparatus in London which managed it, its dockyards and bases, the organization of its crews, the manner in which their responsibilities were divided, the hierarchy of command aboard the vessels and the tasks performed by a ship's company from ordinary seaman to admiral. The ships themselves are described in terms of their ratings and armament, providing insight into the capabilities of the vessels that comprised the most formidable navy of its day, together with discussion of the tactics employed in battle.

The success of the Royal Navy during this period rested on a combination of factors, not least the efficient manner in which it was organized and led. These features, together with advances in ship design, gunnery, discipline and seamanship, were the products of generations of change that enabled the Navy to reach maturity by the beginning of the 19th century.

Combat mission

The roles performed by the Royal Navy were manifold, with its primary function being the defence of the United Kingdom from invasion. It was also required to blockade enemy fleets in port so as to leave the initiative at sea in British hands. By confining the enemy's principal warships to their berths, the Navy was free to harass enemy shipping and enable the Army to conquer overseas possessions, however far flung they might be. The Royal Navy was also responsible for protecting British merchant vessels plying the seas to and from the Continent, across the Atlantic to America, Canada and the West Indies, in and out of the Mediterranean as far as the Levant, and around the Cape of Good Hope to India and the East Indies. In addition, the Navy performed the general task of maintaining a permanent presence at sea, cruising for the purpose of hindering the movements of enemy warships and merchant vessels. The Navy also supported the operations of the Army, whether it was conducting short-term operations, as in the West Indies where ships were required to transport troops for the seizure of particular islands, or where fighting took place over an extended period, as during the Peninsular War (1808–14) when the Navy maintained communication and supply routes between Britain and Wellington's Army in Spain and Portugal. Finally, the Navy was expected to bring the enemy's main fleet to battle and there, if possible, to destroy it.

Defending the coast of southern England entailed constant patrolling, in conjunction with a vigilant watch over the Channel ports, particularly Brest. So long as the enemy's main fleets could be bottled up in port their location

The battle of the Nile, 1–2 August 1798. By destroying the French fleet in Aboukir Bay, Nelson not only isolated – and thus neutralized – Bonaparte's Army in Egypt, but re-established the naval presence in the Mediterranean that Britain had lost in 1796 as a result of the Franco-Spanish alliance of that year. (Philip Haythornthwaite)

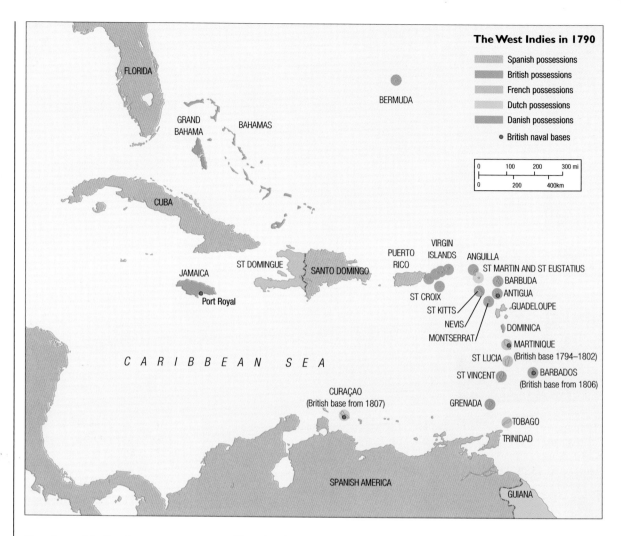

The West Indies in 1790

Spanish possessions
British possessions
French possessions
Dutch possessions
Danish possessions
• British naval bases

| 0 | 100 | 200 | 300 mi |
| 0 | 200 | 400km | |

FLORIDA

BERMUDA

GRAND BAHAMA
BAHAMAS

CUBA

VIRGIN
ISLANDS
PUERTO RICO
ANGUILLA
ST MARTIN AND ST EUSTATIUS
ST DOMINGUE
SANTO DOMINGO
BARBUDA
JAMAICA
ST CROIX
ANTIGUA
Port Royal
ST KITTS
GUADELOUPE
NEVIS
DOMINICA
MONTSERRAT
MARTINIQUE
ST LUCIA (British base 1794–1802)

C A R I B B E A N   S E A

ST VINCENT
BARBADOS
(British base from 1806)

CURAÇAO
(British base from 1807)
GRENADA

TOBAGO
TRINIDAD

SPANISH AMERICA

GUIANA

The seizure of the French sugar islands in the Caribbean played a fundamental part in British naval strategy. Practically every French-held island in the Caribbean was captured by forces conveyed by the Royal Navy, only to be restored to France at the Peace of Amiens in 1802. When war was renewed the following year, a series of British expeditions retook the islands, denying France vital raw materials and the considerable revenue generated by her formerly lucrative West Indian trade.

was, self-evidently, known (whereas, of course, when at sea they could easily elude detection), even if maintaining them in place could not be absolutely assured. Like those on blockade duty, ships assigned to convoy merchant vessels often remained at sea for many months, particularly those assigned to protect trade to and from India, to which a return journey took in the order of six months. Even to North America the journey lasted four to six weeks depending on the winds and current. When conveying troops for operations overseas, the Navy cleared the path of enemy vessels and protected the transports carrying the infantry, cavalry and artillery, which necessarily composed the expeditionary force.

The ultimate aim of the Navy was, however, to seek out the main enemy battle fleet and destroy it, an objective effected only gradually as a result of the six most decisive battles of the period: First of June (1794), St Vincent (1797), Camperdown (1797), Nile (1798), Copenhagen (1801) and Trafalgar (1805). In all but two of these cases (Nile and Copenhagen) the enemy fleet was caught in the open sea and defeated through superior tactics, gunnery and ship handling. At the Nile and at Copenhagen, the British attacked while the French and Danes, respectively, were at anchor and confident of their apparently unassailable position. Yet again, superior British training, discipline and firepower proved more than a match for their adversaries. In the case of Trafalgar, the defeat inflicted on the combined Franco-Spanish fleet proved so crippling that it prevented the French from ever again seriously

challenging British naval supremacy, and constituted such a mortal blow to Spanish maritime power as to bring a definitive end to her position as a great naval power – a process which had begun as long ago as the defeat of the Armada in 1588.

Recruitment and the press

The younger sons of the middle class – as opposed to the aristocracy, which preferred the Army since only there could wealth secure an instant commission – entered the Navy as aspiring officers, and often did so from a young age. A boy of 12, for instance, might begin in the capacity of a captain's servant, which only meant that he was in effect a trainee and not an actual servant. After a few years at sea he could become a midshipman, a type of non-commissioned officer immediately below the rank of lieutenant. A few men spent time at the Royal Naval Academy, Portsmouth, but most young officers received their education and training aboard ship under the tutelage of the ship's schoolmaster or chaplain, who guided them in mathematics, navigation and other subjects. Once he reached the age of 20 (and the required six years' service at sea), a midshipman took the lieutenant's examination, the passing of which entitled him to that commissioned rank and enabled him thereafter to work his way up the ladder of promotion. While this could be an extremely slow process, in wartime it was not necessarily so, owing to deaths in combat and, above all, from sickness and disease. One could also achieve promotion through patronage – what contemporaries called 'interest'. Since, in marked contrast to the Army, a commission could not be purchased nor promotion secured by financial means, making the best use of one's personal connections was the next best option.

In theory the Navy, like the Army, was a volunteer force, but with the Navy's worldwide commitments always increasing and its ship-building programme seemingly perpetual, Britain was chronically short of men, with only 65,000 men available in 1794, gradually rising to 140,000 men in 1815. Losses, of

HMS *Shannon* captures USS *Chesapeake*, 1 June 1813, in one of the most celebrated frigate actions of the War of 1812. In a mere matter of minutes, Captain Philip Broke of the *Shannon* systematically pummelled his adversary's port side with accurate and highly destructive fire, killing the quartermasters, disabling the wheel and forcing *Chesapeake* to luff up out of control. Already seriously wounded in the opening salvo, James Lawrence, the American captain, was struck again, and while lying in the cockpit to receive medical care issued his famous order, 'Don't give up the ship!' But it was to no avail: the *Shannon* raked the stricken vessel, and when exploding ammunition cleared away those standing on *Chesapeake's* quarterdeck, Broke personally led a boarding party and seized the ship after a brief, though bloody hand-to-hand encounter in which Broke was clubbed by a musket butt and received a serious blow from a cutlass. (Stratford Archive)

Boarding action. Although such attacks often took place when two ships stood abreast, often secured together by hooks or chains, they could also involve ships' boats, as depicted here. A midshipman, dressed in black coat and round hat, urges both sailors and marines forward into the ferocity of hand-to-hand combat. Boats, which could be rowed or sailed, were stored on beams in the ship's waist and hoisted by tackles from the yards. In addition to boarding actions, boats served numerous other purposes, such as carrying supplies, turning a ship under windless conditions, performing cutting-out expeditions, providing communication with other vessels, and landing sailors and marines. (Angus Konstam)

course, had to be replaced, and could result from a combination of factors: combat deaths and injury, disease, desertion and injuries sustained in the ordinary course of what was a hazardous duty even without an enemy in sight. The number of volunteers was never sufficient for the nation's needs because conditions aboard ship were so poor, with considerable periods spent at sea, dreadful food, harsh discipline and low pay.

A solution was found in the practice of impressment, whereby the state maintained the right to seize men for service as the need arose. Even contemporaries regarded this legacy of medieval times as an assault on the liberties of free men – not to mention an inefficient method of raising crews – but as Parliament refused to introduce conscription either in the Army or the Navy, the practice was regularly and shamelessly employed. Men in port towns were the most vulnerable to impressment, for they were the most likely to have served at sea, usually aboard merchant vessels or as discharged sailors from the Navy. Some men were exempt: men of sufficient means, i.e. 'gentlemen', seamen already serving in the Royal Navy, fishermen, tradesmen, apprentices, those under 18 or over 55, and a few other categories of men. Anyone else who appeared reasonably fit could potentially fall prey to a press gang, a party of ruffians assembled by a lieutenant, who proceeded to collar those who looked of some use aboard ship. Not only were men taken on the streets, but merchant ships were often stopped as they returned to home waters and stripped of their best sailors. Men were often offered the chance to 'volunteer' so that they could claim the bounty (this varied throughout the wars from between £1 10s and £10) offered to those who willingly enlisted, and thus it is difficult to determine precisely how many men joined the Navy as genuine volunteers. Such men may have accounted for as little as a quarter of a ship's company.

Organization

Organization of the Navy

The highest form of operational organization in the Navy was the fleet. Under normal circumstances, a fleet was formed into a single line before action commenced, and in some instances broke apart in the course of the fighting into duels between individual ships. For this reason a subordinate admiral, whether in command of a division or a squadron, did not play a vital role in combat. He was advised by Admiralty instructions to 'be particularly attentive in observing that a ship which carries his flag, and all the squadrons and divisions under his orders, preserve very correctly their station in whatever line or order of sailing the fleet may be formed'.

The manner in which an admiral divided his fleet lay entirely at his own discretion, though he generally apportioned at least ten of his ships of the line to a squadron. These could then be sub-divided into divisions while at sea or to function in this form in battle.

Squadrons were approximately of equal strength, with those at Trafalgar being 13 and 14 ships, respectively. In 1807, Admiral Gambier had three equal squadrons of ten ships, with each squadron divided into two divisions, under a rear-admiral or commodore. While cruising, fleets did not usually organize themselves according to the line of battle that they assumed when in the presence of the enemy. They might cruise in two parallel lines of approximately equal strength, a mile or more apart, with each line's vessels sailing bow to stern with two or three cables (a cable being 100 fathoms, or 200 yards) between them, or in line abreast, with ships sailing on parallel courses. In order to maintain communications between the various divisions, frigates were positioned at various points around the fleet and lookouts kept aloft at their stations.

The vast majority of ships in the Royal Navy were assigned to one of the main fleets, which were distributed around the world. Some vessels served exclusively on convoy duty, while others, on individual missions from the Admiralty, were not attached to a particular fleet. Each fleet was led by a commander-in-chief – always a very senior admiral. While some squadrons were formed for specific purposes and often bore the names of their commanders, fleets were normally

The primary function of the sailing warship, which was defined by the number of guns she carried, was to engage the enemy. Guns, today commonly referred to as 'cannon' but more correctly as 'great' or 'long' guns, were simply weapons consisting of an iron tube, without rifling, mounted on a heavy carriage with four small wooden wheels on fixed axles. A gunner could raise or lower the elevation of his weapon by +10 degrees or –5 degrees by inserting or removing a quoin, or wooden wedge. The carriage itself could be aimed to a limited extent by pulling on the gun tackles – a series of ropes fastened to the sides of the carriage and secured to the deck. Handspikes and crowbars were also employed in manhandling the gun into the desired position. Every gun was commanded by a 'gun captain' whose men varied in number according to the size of the gun. If a ship were firing from one side alone, the crew from the unengaged side would assist the men on the opposite side of the gun deck, so increasing the rapidity of fire. (Royal Naval Museum)

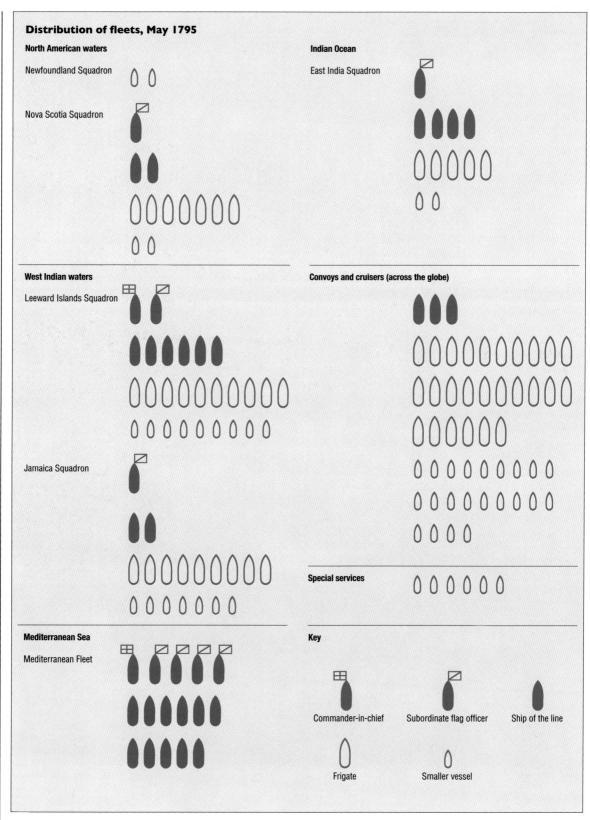

Distribution of fleets, May 1795

North American waters

Newfoundland Squadron

Nova Scotia Squadron

Indian Ocean

East India Squadron

West Indian waters

Leeward Islands Squadron

Jamaica Squadron

Convoys and cruisers (across the globe)

Special services

Mediterranean Sea

Mediterranean Fleet

Key

Commander-in-chief

Subordinate flag officer

Ship of the line

Frigate

Smaller vessel

This shows the number of vessels assigned to the fleets, though the actual strength *in situ* could vary. Note that the Channel and North Seas fleets are not shown.

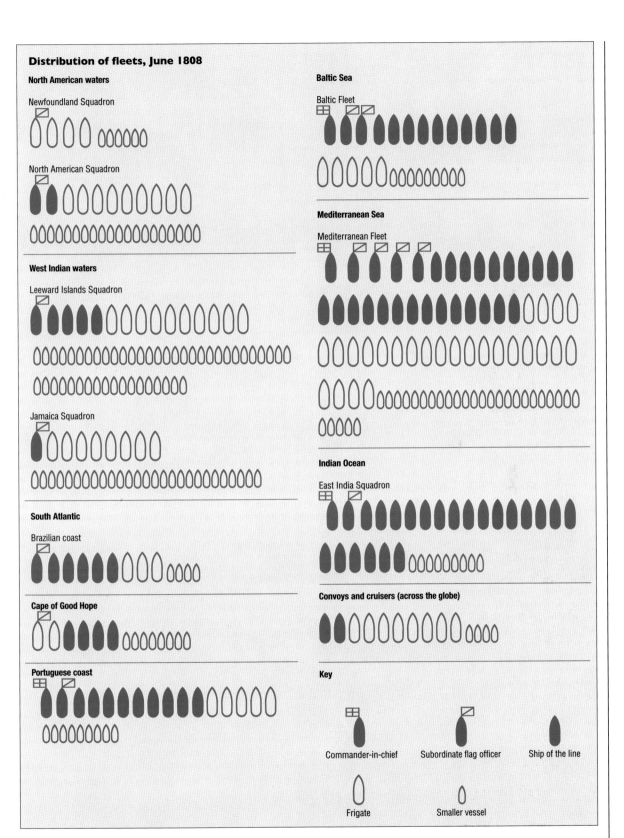

Distribution of fleets, June 1808

North American waters

Newfoundland Squadron

North American Squadron

West Indian waters

Leeward Islands Squadron

Jamaica Squadron

South Atlantic

Brazilian coast

Cape of Good Hope

Portuguese coast

Baltic Sea

Baltic Fleet

Mediterranean Sea

Mediterranean Fleet

Indian Ocean

East India Squadron

Convoys and cruisers (across the globe)

Key

Commander-in-chief

Subordinate flag officer

Ship of the line

Frigate

Smaller vessel

Given the sheer size of the Royal Navy it is easy to assume that the defence of the nation could be taken for granted. In reality, Britain's naval requirements demanded the presence of its fleets across the world's oceans, and hence the Channel, though well defended, was patrolled by only a fraction of the Navy's resources.

Fleet organization

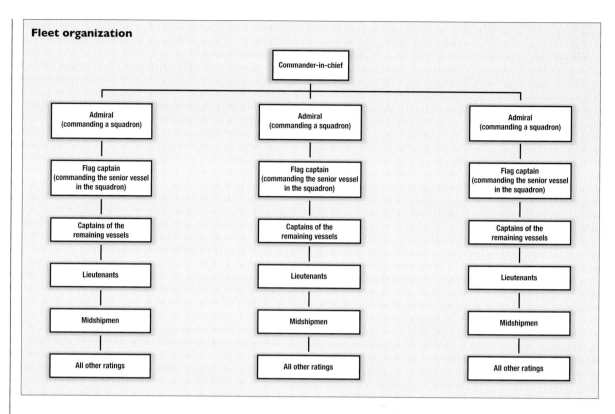

All fleets were divided into divisions or squadrons, usually led by vice- or rear-admirals or commodores, with fleet commands normally held only by full admirals. Every ship was commanded by a captain, themselves supported by lieutenants and midshipmen.

assigned to a particular stretch of ocean – a sort of geographical area of responsibility. The actual area covered was not always perfectly defined, so that, for instance, the Mediterranean Fleet served as far as the coast of Portugal, while the Channel Fleet cruised well into the Bay of Biscay as far as the northern coast of Spain. Needless to say, the strengths of the various fleets varied according to the relative importance of their roles and responsibilities. Thus, the Channel Fleet, whose principal function was to defend the southern coast of England and whose secondary role was to blockade Brest, was invariably maintained on a strong footing, whereas the West Indian fleets were generally scaled down once the French were driven from the Caribbean. The Newfoundland and Nova Scotia fleets were nearly always small, with little to do until war broke out with the United States in June 1812. In all, there were seven or eight main fleets with titles based on their respective geographical areas, in addition to numerous single ships and detached or independent squadrons, usually composed of frigates and smaller craft.

The Channel Fleet

The Channel Fleet served as the principal arm of the nation's defence. It not only cruised the waterway between Britain and the Continent in order to prevent invasion, but kept constant watch over the French ports of Brest, Le Havre, Cherbourg, Lorient, Rochefort and others, engaging whenever possible vessels which ventured out. Brest was the principal enemy port in this area, but where sufficient numbers of ships were available the Channel Fleet could blockade the other French ports, as well as Ferrol on the north-west coast of Spain. In 1804, the fleet was to have 20 ships of the line to serve off Brest, with another seven off Rochefort, seven others off Ferrol and three more off the Portuguese and Spanish coasts. This ensured that no enemy could venture past Gibraltar without detection. The main bases of the Channel Fleet were Portsmouth and Plymouth, and it used the anchorages at Spithead, St Helens and elsewhere on the south coast of England.

In 1795 the Channel Fleet consisted of 26 ships of the line, plus 17 frigates. In 1800 it had three first rates, 11 second rates and 33 other ships of the line. With its frigates and other vessels it numbered in total 72 ships and smaller craft. In 1805 it numbered 35 ships of the line and 16 frigates, but by 1812 it was down to just 15 ships of the line, 14 frigates and ten other smaller vessels. Since the Brest Fleet was not present at Trafalgar it was never destroyed, and hence the strength of the Channel Fleet necessarily remained high. It fought one large action, at the First of June 1794, but notwithstanding French losses of six ships the remainder of the opposing fleet reached Brest and thereafter had to be continuously watched.

The Irish Squadron

Based principally at Cork, in southern Ireland, the Irish Squadron existed to protect trade moving westwards across the Atlantic, as well as to defend Ireland from invasion, though its smaller numbers obliged it to depend on assistance from the Channel Fleet as circumstances required. In 1797 the squadron had 16 ships, only one of which was a line of battle ship, the others being frigates and sloops. This force was reduced two years later to 12 ships. In 1805 it had 23 ships, of which 12 were frigates and eight were sloops. In 1812, with naval supremacy achieved, the Irish Squadron consisted of only 13 ships, with no complement of line of battle ships.

North Sea Fleet

The second most important major home command was the North Sea Fleet, whose name is slightly misleading since part of its area of responsibility extended into the Channel as far as the Dutch and Belgian coasts. In 1797 it numbered 56 ships, including 20 of the line. It was with this fleet that Admiral Duncan fought and won the battle of Camperdown in that year. Attached to the North Sea Fleet was the Downs Squadron, which protected the entrance to the Channel. When war began in 1803 this squadron and others were combined into a single fleet, which two years later, in the year of Trafalgar, reached a strength of 80 ships, including 11 of the line and 20 frigates, the whole divided into five squadrons, with responsibilities for blockading the French port of Boulogne, and the Texel and the Scheldt, the main entrances to the Dutch ports. The strength of the fleet fluctuated greatly over the years, with 34 ships in the Downs Squadron in 1807, of which one was a ship of the line. Eight vessels were based at Yarmouth, but none larger than a sloop; seven small vessels hailed from Sheerness; and 15 from Leith. In 1812, the Downs Squadron had 31 ships, but none of the line or frigates. At Yarmouth there were eight

As in the British Army, where a certain flexibility enabled the number of brigades composing a division to vary according to circumstances, the same principle applied in the Royal Navy, in which a fleet could consist of a fluctuating number of vessels depending on the resources available, the nature of the task to be fulfilled, detachments made for auxiliary operations or the acquisition of supplies, and other factors. Nor did a fleet necessarily operate as single, consolidated force. The vast expanse patrolled by the Channel Fleet required its commander to allocate a proportion of his vessels to blockade duty while the bulk of his ships of the line remained either in port or at sea, ready to confront a rival fleet when required. Similarly, whereas at Trafalgar Nelson assembled virtually the whole of the Mediterranean Fleet, his force at the Nile seven years earlier had comprised only a squadron from the same fleet (then under St Vincent), though naval historiography, both contemporary and modern, often refers to his 'fleet'.

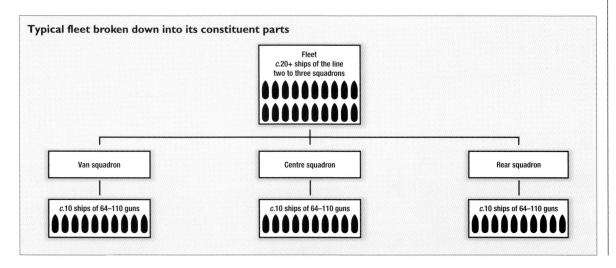

Typical fleet broken down into its constituent parts

Fleet
c.20+ ships of the line
two to three squadrons

Van squadron	Centre squadron	Rear squadron
c.10 ships of 64–110 guns	c.10 ships of 64–110 guns	c.10 ships of 64–110 guns

ships, half of them sloops. The force watching the Texel and the Scheldt had 53 ships, of which 27 were of the line, five frigates and 12 sloops. Fourteen ships, including two frigates and four sloops, were based at Leith.

The Baltic Fleet

While important in British naval strategy, the Baltic Fleet was not always on station in great numbers, but rather was augmented as circumstances required. This was particularly true in 1801, when formation of the League of Armed Neutrality involving Denmark, Sweden and Russia led the Admiralty to dispatch a powerful fleet under Sir Hyde Parker, with Nelson as second in command. The fleet consisted of 21 ships of the line, 11 frigates and ships of 50 guns, plus a large armada of gunboats, brigs, cutters, schooners and luggers. In fact, it was more of a fleet assigned a special mission than a permanent fixture with a geographical designation. It was with this fleet that Nelson won the battle of Copenhagen.

The Baltic Fleet again assumed importance in 1807, when Admiral Gambier was dispatched with a fleet of 17 ships of the line to force the Danes into surrendering their ships in the wake of the accommodation between France and Russia in July. In the following year a permanent Baltic Fleet was established in reply to the French establishment of the Continental System and the belligerence of Denmark following Gambier's seizure of its fleet. In 1812 the Baltic Fleet numbered 39 ships, including ten of the line, six frigates and 14 sloops.

The Mediterranean Fleet

The Mediterranean Fleet, second only in importance to the Channel Fleet, was a vital component of the Royal Navy, for the Mediterranean held important British strategic interests. The fleet was always led by a senior and experienced admiral whose primary responsibility lay in maintaining a close blockade on the principal French port, Toulon, and the Spanish port of Cadiz. This fleet fought off the Hyères Islands in 1795, and in three other battles of much

Action between the USS *Argus* and HMS *Pelican*, 14 August 1813. The American brig, cruising in British coastal waters, carried out the most destructive cruise of any US warship during the conflict with Britain, taking 19 merchant ships between the English Channel and southern Ireland, an area known as the Western Approaches. The *Pelican*, observing the burning wreck of one of *Argus*'s recent triumphs, gave chase, using her carronades to destroy her opponent's main braces and after running rigging. This rendered *Argus* unmanageable, thus enabling *Pelican* to rake the stricken vessel until it struck its colours after 45 minutes' resistance. (Stratford Archive)

greater significance – Cape St Vincent in 1797, the Nile in 1798 and Trafalgar in 1805. Like the other geographical commands, the fleet designated for service in the Mediterranean did not always confine itself to what ought to have been a clearly defined area. Thus, St Vincent and Trafalgar were fought west of Gibraltar; in the latter case Nelson even chased Admiral Villeneuve across the Atlantic before following him back to European waters. The Mediterranean Fleet varied in strength as circumstances required. In 1795 it had 31 ships, including five first and second rates, 11 third rates, and 11 fifth and sixth rates. In 1797 it surpassed even the strength of the Channel Fleet, with 62 ships, including 23 of the line, 24 frigates and ten sloops. By 1812 – years after the decisive victory at Trafalgar – it was even larger, with 90 ships, consisting of 29 of the line, the same number of frigates, and 26 sloops.

The West Indies

Whereas during the American Revolutionary War the West Indies had been a very active theatre of naval operations, particularly in the later stages of the conflict, this was not so during the French Revolutionary and Napoleonic Wars, when the French did not maintain a fleet there, particularly after the fall of Martinique. The British naval forces in the Caribbean were divided into two commands, one for Jamaica and the other for the Leeward Islands. The former was based at Port Royal. Its principal function was to combat privateers and provide convoy service in the western Caribbean. When the war began in 1793, the Jamaica Squadron consisted of a 50-gun ship, three 32-gun frigates, four sloops and a schooner. In 1795 there were 19 ships on the station – three ships of the line, two fourth rates, six fifth rates, a sixth rate and three schooners. Two years later the station had 31 ships, including seven of the line, 15 frigates and seven sloops. This was increased by 1805 to 51 ships, including three of the line, 14 frigates and 24 sloops. In 1812, with all of the French West Indian possessions in British hands, the station amounted to only 19 ships, of which one was a ship of the line, eight were frigates and the rest smaller vessels.

The Leeward Islands Squadron was based at Antigua and Barbados, though it could also use Martinique and St Lucia once those French colonies had been captured. At the beginning of the war this force numbered nine ships of the

Launching a ship of the line. Ships of this size took years to construct, either in the Royal dockyards or in private yards. Much remains to be done to the ship depicted here, which must now be 'fitted out' with three vertical masts and a bowsprit, together with all the yards, booms, and gaffs to which sails will eventually be attached. Fully fitted ships were festooned with miles of rigging – all the ropes, cables and chains used to support the masts and spars and to raise, lower and adjust sails and yards – together with the tackle – pulley blocks, eyebolts and other apparatus used to hold or adjust them. After the rigging came all the ancillary equipment, including the rudder and wheel, anchors and their cables, capstans, the ship's boats, the galley stove, pumps and other equipment. The ship's armament was also added, together with the tools and tackle associated with it. The interior of the ship had also to be finished, including the cabins and quarters, galley, magazine and store rooms. Once complete, the ship was formally commissioned, at which point all her stores were added and a crew assembled to man her. (Royal Naval Museum)

line and 14 smaller ships and vessels, though it was increased within a year by three more ships of the line and seven other vessels, together with a large convoy of troops with which began the campaigns for the capture of the French West Indian possessions. In 1795 the Leeward Islands Squadron consisted of 26 ships, including eight third rates, ten frigates, six sloops and other vessels. In 1797 it numbered 44 ships – nine of the line, 16 frigates and 11 sloops. Thereafter the fleet was gradually decreased as a result of the capture of most of the French colonies. By 1801, just before a short-lived peace was signed at Amiens, the fleet was down to just 26 ships and vessels, including one of the line, nine frigates, seven sloops and other craft.

As the settlement at Amiens restored most French possessions, when war resumed in 1803 the fleet in the West Indies had to be increased so as to enable it to capture these islands all over again. In 1805 it numbered six of the line, 13 frigates and the same number of sloops, but by 1812 it had again been reduced, owing to the fact that by 1810 all the colonies of France and her allies had been retaken. Royal Navy warships in the West Indies totalled 27, including one of the line, five frigates and 13 sloops.

The North American Station

Two squadrons were maintained off the American coast, with bases at Halifax, Nova Scotia, and at Newfoundland. These were considered minor areas of responsibility, for the United States remained neutral until 1812. When war with France began in 1793, the Halifax Squadron had only four ships and vessels, none of which exceeded 32 guns; the Newfoundland Squadron had one 64-gun ship, three frigates and five sloops. Nor did Royal Navy strength grow by an appreciable degree: five ships in 1797, seven two years later, 13 in 1805, and 12 in 1812. In 1795, the Halifax Squadron had ten ships, of which three were third rates. In 1800 this rose to 13, including two third rates. The number fell five years later to only eight ships, none of which were larger than frigates. As a result of the war with the United States, however, the waters along the

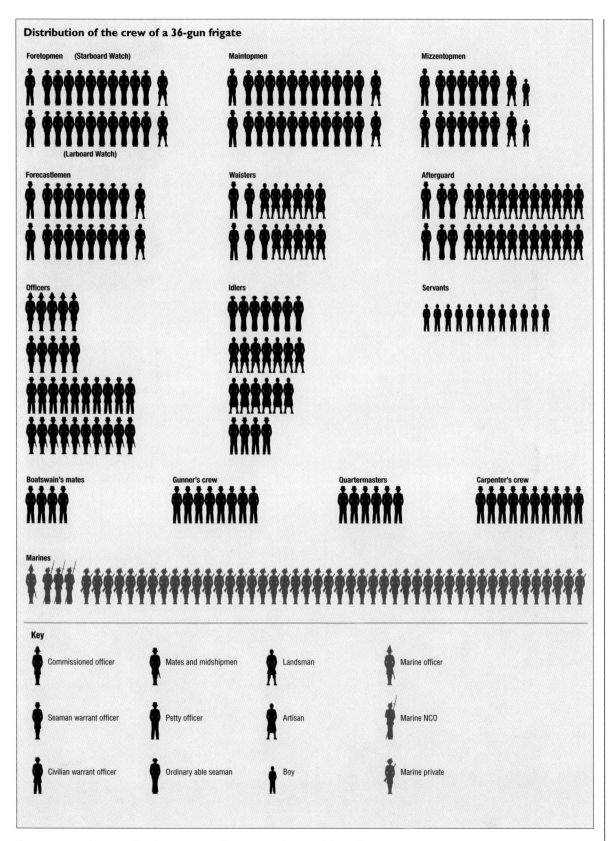

Distribution of the crew of a 36-gun frigate

Every man on a ship was assigned a station based on aptitude, fitness, training and experience.

American and Canadian coasts grew in importance, and by the late summer of 1812 the station had 25 ships, including one of the line, eight frigates and seven sloops. This increased again by the following year, when the North American station numbered 60 ships, including 11 third rates, 16 fifth rates and 25 sloops.

East Indies and the Cape

Ships assigned to these stations carried out raids in the East Indies and protected merchantmen in convoys bound for Europe. The East India Squadron in particular mostly protected trade originating from India. In the first year of the war it numbered 13 ships, including five third rates. By 1797 it had 32 ships, including ten of the line, 17 frigates and four sloops. Two years later this number had declined to 17, rising again to 23, including 17 of the line, by 1803. In 1805 it numbered 29 ships, including eight of the line. In 1812 the fleet was 24 ships strong, including one of the line.

Organization of the crew

No vessel could operate properly without an adequate system for the organization of its crew. Ships often carried considerable numbers of men, who could not be expected to perform usefully as a single entity. A first rate, for instance, contained over 800 men, and the larger frigates over 300, with some proportion being unwilling occupants, while others were unable to read, disaffected or lazy. There were also some affected by illness, tiredness or drunkenness, or who harboured grievances of one sort or another. In the face of all these obstacles, the ship, in all its complexity as something of a small floating village, had to be managed. As the same crew might remain aboard the same vessel – in extremely cramped conditions – year after year, with consequently little in the way of new social contacts, an exceptional degree of discipline and intelligent organization was required to keep the ship running efficiently.

The crew was divided into groups and assigned specific tasks, often several at a time depending on the mission of the ship at any given time. A sailor could be assigned to a specific part of the rigging, serve a particular gun during battle, or work the pumps if necessary. When the ship docked or disembarked, he might play some other role, and even this might change – for instance to duties connected with his mess at mealtimes – depending on which watch it happened to be. Whatever his responsibilities, usually assigned to him by the first lieutenant who first considered the man's aptitude and fitness for the job – and these could be a dozen or two – a seaman was expected to perform them quickly and efficiently.

It was the first lieutenant's responsibility to ensure that enough men were on duty at any given time so that the ship was safe and functioning well. He normally divided the crew, therefore, into two or three watches. The majority of ships used the two-watch system, which resulted in nearly every man belonging to one or the other, in nearly equal numbers, with the watches known as larboard and starboard. If both watches were on deck, those men assigned to the larboard watch might be responsible for the ropes and line of their side of the ship (the left-hand side as one faces the bow), while those of the starboard watch manned the other side.

Boarding. In the frenzy of combat firearms could not be reloaded – hence the preference amongst most seamen for edged weapons. The attackers (right), largely armed with cutlasses – apart from the tomahawk-wielding sailor in the foreground – are led by an officer, identifiable by his bicorn hat worn 'fore-and-aft'; that is, with the peaks to front and rear, as opposed to 'amidships', or side-to-side. The defenders (left) favour the pike which, while often effective for repelling boarders, proved a liability if an assailant managed to parry a thrust and skirt past the point of the weapon. (Royal Naval Museum)

Sailors floating on debris. Contrary to popular belief, ships rarely sank in battle; storms and shoals were the principal culprits. When a ship did sink, panic normally ensued, as one sailor described: 'All hands were now struck with consternation and dismay, and everything was enveloped in uncertainty and gloom. The officers, hoarse by so much exertion of voice, issued their orders hesitatingly, and in vain. Subordination, the first and most important branch in naval discipline, seemed for the time being suspended in every man ... In vain did the captain call out for all hands to remain on board till day break, when all would be saved; everyone acted to the best of his own judgement.' (Philip Haythornthwaite)

Idlers

Those men who were not a part of one of the watches were known as idlers, the name given to those whose services were needed on a constant basis during the day, and therefore were not expected to keep any of the night watches, unless of course all hands were summoned on deck at night. Idlers constituted about 7 per cent of the crew on a first rate and about 10 per cent on a sixth rate. Idlers included the master at arms and the various corporals, the armourer, sailmaker, cooper and the mates working along with them, the yeoman of the boatswain's, carpenter's and gunner's store rooms. Other idlers included the cook and his assistants, butchers, hairdressers, barbers, tailors, pursers, poulterers, the first lieutenant's secretary, the purser's steward and various officers' servants (not domestic servants – though they did perform menial services from time to time – but rather young officer hopefuls). Some of the marines would fall under the category of idler, as well, plus tailors, shoemakers, painters and bakers.

Topmen

Apart from the idlers, the rest of the crew were assigned part of the ship for which they were responsible, a designation that gave rise to nicknames which reflected the area in which they carried out their tasks. Thus, the topmen, the most skilled seamen, worked aloft in the masts and amongst the rigging. Ships of the line had three types of topmen, one each for the fore (forwardmost), main (middle) and mizzen (rearmost) masts. Aboard smaller ships, the mizzentopmen formed part of the afterguard, which will be described later. The topmen, maintopmen, foretopmen and mizzentopmen had to be extremely fit and agile, for they had to perform work in the highest masts, sometimes in the face of high winds and rain and a rolling ship. Their numbers varied, but, for instance, aboard the *San Domingo*, a 74, there were 25 foretopmen, 27 maintopmen and 25 mizzentopmen in each watch. Each group was led by a petty officer, known as the captain of the foretop, mizzentop or maintop, as appropriate.

Forecastle men

Owing to their specialist abilities and knowledge, the topmen enjoyed a virtual monopoly on work aloft, with the remainder of the crew rarely permitted (or indeed able) to go into the rigging. The forecastle men worked towards the front of the ship, known as the forecastle (pronounced 'foc-sul'), and handled, amongst other equipment, the anchors. They were often the oldest and heaviest sailors, since they were depended upon for both skill and strength, not dexterity; nor were they required to act with particular swiftness, like those in the tops. A 36-gun frigate contained about 20 forecastle men, all but perhaps two of whom were petty officers or able seamen, led by a captain of the forecastle for each watch.

Afterguard and waisters

The afterguard, which worked on the quarterdeck and poop, was composed of men who almost never went aloft, except perhaps to help furl the mainsail (pronounced 'mainsul'), and were effectively used for their brute strength, such as for pulling and hauling. Aboard a 36-gun frigate there were about 28 such men, perhaps half a dozen being able seamen, which is to say men possessing more skills than ordinary seamen. The waisters possessed the fewest skills of the men on deck, being composed of the least useful landsmen, whom some of the crew regarded as less than true sailors. Waisters performed the least interesting and most onerous work on the main, or gun, deck and sometimes assisted with the lines and ropes. A 74-gun ship might contain about 30 waisters in each watch.

These six parts of the ship (three types of topmen, forecastle men, afterguard and waisters), accounted for about half the ship's company, the remainder being officers, marines, boys and servants.

Divisions

Large and medium-sized ships were also organized into divisions to enable the officers to administer the ship's company along logical administrative and social lines, as opposed to the system previously described, which concerned their duties only. According to the Admiralty Regulations and Instructions, the captain, aided by his officers, was to:

Divide the ship's company, exclusive of the marines, into as many divisions as there are lieutenants allowed to the ship; the divisions are to be equal in number to each other, and the men are to be taken equally from the different stations in which they are watched. A lieutenant is to command each division; he is to have under his orders as many master's mates and midshipmen as the number on board, being equally divided, will admit; he is to sub-divide his division into as many sub-divisions as there are mates and midshipmen fit to command under his orders.

The division enabled the captain and his officers to monitor the health and welfare of the ship's company. Proper sanitation aboard the ship was essential in order to ward off sickness and disease, and thus the officers inspected the clothing and bedding of their division, and were responsible for seeing that the men did not swear or get drunk – no simple task. Petty officers and midshipmen kept lists of the men for whom they were responsible within a given division, each list indicating every sailor's duty and the number of his hammock. When in port, those in charge of a division mustered their men each evening, and conducted inspections for health and cleanliness every Sunday morning.

Heaving the line, one of the innumerable tasks performed by sailors in the operation of a ship. Weighing anchor, for instance, required the combined strength of much of a ship's company, not only to turn the capstan which raised the anchor (of which ships of the line carried several), but to coil the massive cables as they were hoisted aboard. At the same time, much of the remaining crew would be busy setting sail and thereafter make more, or shorten, sail depending on weather conditions and the captain's instructions. (Stratford Archive)

Officers

Midshipman

Midshipmen were usually volunteers, aged between 14 and 18, eager to be commissioned as lieutenants – the first rung on the ladder of promotion in naval service. Some, however, were men promoted from the lower deck, such that midshipmen could be considerably older – up to perhaps 40 – having failed to pass the exam for lieutenant. Once aged 14 or older, a midshipman held the same rank as a petty officer, while younger midshipmen held the equivalent rank of an able seaman.

Midshipmen oversaw the work performed by most of the crew of lesser rank, and kept the watch system, whether two or three, functioning on time. The senior midshipman of the watch stood on the quarterdeck, the second on the forecastle, and the third abaft the mizzen mast. Others, of less experience, answered to their superiors and carried out all manner of tasks such as taking and recording soundings, notifying the officer of the watch of anything of note, and marking the log slate. Using sextants or quadrants, midshipmen would also record the ship's position at noon, being careful to take this and other pertinent information down in their journals, which the captain would later inspect. Midshipmen oversaw signalling, commanded the boats and worked aloft, situating themselves, according to directions from a lieutenant, in one of the mast tops, where they supervised the furling and reefing of sails.

Each of the ship's divisions was assigned a midshipman who was responsible for numerous tasks, such as ensuring that the men had clean clothing, that the ill were accounted for on the sick list and reported to the sick bay, and that hammocks were stowed after use. Midshipmen could inflict minor punishments on seamen, usually in the form of blows delivered by a knotted rope. Sailors with years of experience behind them, and sometimes considerably older than a midshipman, had no option but to endure the reprimands and punishments of mere teenagers.

A ship contained four types of officers, the most senior being commissioned officers – the captain and his lieutenants – who were appointed by the Admiralty, with midshipmen training to become lieutenants. Warrant officers were next in importance, and consisted of the master, who was responsible for the navigation of the ship, the chaplain, who performed church services, the purser, who stocked, supplied and managed the ship's stores, and the surgeon, who served as a physician as well as a surgeon proper. Standing officers – so-called because they remained with their ship even when it was de-commissioned – consisted of the boatswain, who supervised all the work conducted above decks, the gunner, who looked after the ship's armament on a day-to-day basis and managed the guns during battle, and the carpenter, who cared for the yards, masts, hull and wooden fittings. Last came petty officers, consisting of men with various specialized skills.

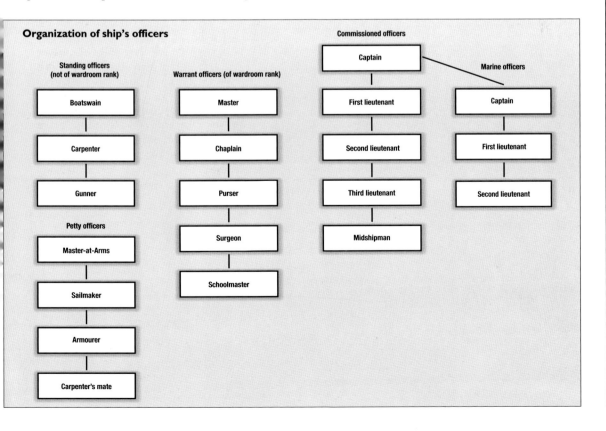

Organization of ship's officers

Standing officers (not of wardroom rank)	Warrant officers (of wardroom rank)	Commissioned officers	Marine officers
		Captain	
Boatswain	Master	First lieutenant	Captain
Carpenter	Chaplain	Second lieutenant	First lieutenant
Gunner	Purser	Third lieutenant	Second lieutenant
Petty officers	Surgeon	Midshipman	
Master-at-Arms	Schoolmaster		
Sailmaker			
Armourer			
Carpenter's mate			

One seaman described in his memoirs how:

We had a midshipman on board of a wickedly mischievous disposition, whose sole delight was to insult the feelings of seamen and furnish pretexts to get them punished … He was a youth of not more than 12 or 13 years of age; I have often seen him get on to the carriage of a gun, call a man to him, and kick him about the thighs and body, and with his feet would beat him about the head; and these, though prime seamen, at the same time dared not murmur.

Prior to battle, a midshipman would see that all the guns, powder cartridges and associated equipment were ready for use. When a ship stood in harbour, a specified number of midshipmen would be assigned to work around the clock in shifts, supervising the upper deck. As a midshipman was an aspiring officer, he spent what time remained between watches studying mathematics, navigation, trigonometry and seamanship, as well as writing in his journals. After about six years' service, by which time he would be about 19, a midshipman would take his examination for lieutenant.

Lieutenant

While lieutenants with sufficient experience commanded one of various types of small vessels such as sloops, armed cutters, brigs or schooners, they are best known as the group of officers immediately junior in rank to the captain. A lieutenant was expected to carry out the orders of the captain or more senior lieutenants quickly and intelligently, whether serving as the officer of the watch or in some other capacity. Specifically, he was to ensure that the ship sailed according to the course and direction dictated by the captain, and remain attentive lest rigging and sails suffer damage from a sudden shift in the direction and strength of the wind. According to Admiralty Regulations, the lieutenant of the watch was to remain on deck in a constant state of vigilance:

To see that the men are alert and attentive to their duty; that every precaution is taken to prevent accidents from squalls, or sudden gusts of winds; and that the ship is as perfectly prepared for battle as circumstances will admit.

A lieutenant was also responsible for the conduct of the midshipmen, mates and seamen under him, ensuring that they all carried out their duties properly. The senior lieutenant on duty was immediately to call the captain on deck if the weather suddenly changed, or if some other pressing matter required his attention.

Numbers of officers, 1803–15													
	1803	1804	1805	1806	1807	1808	1809	1810	1811	1812	1813	1814	1815
Admirals	45	41	50	55	52	48	46	49	65	62	64	65	70
Vice-admirals	36	32	36	50	57	55	59	61	60	65	69	68	73
Rear-admirals	51	50	63	56	50	58	71	60	56	60	68	76	76
Captains	668	673	639	617	693	700	689	725	753	777	802	798	824
Commanders	413	409	422	416	502	501	543	608	558	566	602	628	762
Lieutenants	2,480	2,457	2,472	2,437	2,728	2,912	3,036	3,114	3,071	3,163	3,268	3,285	3,211
Masters	529	541	556	541	429	549	491	501	544	567	629	674	666

Trafalgar. By breaking the Franco-Spanish line in two places, Nelson was able to isolate Admiral Villeneuve's centre and rear, thus compensating for the allies' numerical superiority. (Philip Haythornthwaite)

Apart from the smallest ships, aboard which only one or two lieutenants served, each ship had a first lieutenant, whose seniority, based on experience, entitled him to the post of second in command. As such he was to report directly to the captain respecting the management of the ship and its crew. He ensured that watch and quarter bills were implemented correctly, which required him to list where all officers, seamen and marines were to be positioned when on watch or in action. The list also laid down the responsibilities to be undertaken by each man so as to cover all eventualities, such as manning the pumps, fighting fires, serving in or leading a boarding party, and sail-handling. The first lieutenant normally did not keep watches, but might be called on deck as needed by the officer of the watch. During battle the first lieutenant stood with the captain on the quarterdeck, and in the event of the captain being injured or killed, command immediately devolved upon the first lieutenant.

The more junior lieutenants each commanded a gun deck in action and oversaw the firing of the guns. With the assistance of midshipmen and quarter gunners, the lieutenant was responsible for seeing that the gun crews always had powder and shot to hand and that the men handling and firing the guns did not abandon their posts under the pressure of enemy fire. Any of the lieutenants not assigned to a particular gun deck would command the guns on the forecastle or quarter deck, or were positioned on the poop deck and given charge of signalling in the capacity of communications officer.

Master and commander

This rank was assigned to officers who commanded vessels smaller than a sixth rate, which is to say sloops and brigs. By the second year of the war, in 1794, the rank was replaced by that of commander, which was effectively the same as a captain of a larger vessel, the only distinction being that a commander was responsible for fewer men and guns.

Captain

A captain (or 'post captain', which distinguished the position from that of 'commander' who was effectively a 'captain' already, but merely of a small vessel) always commanded a ship of sixth rate class and above. These men normally rose from the rank of commander, though those who demonstrated particular promise or who had distinguished themselves might only hold the rank of commander very briefly before becoming captain. The captain was junior only to his superior squadron commander, who held the rank of commodore or admiral. Thus, aboard his own ship, the captain reigned supreme. He was ultimately responsible for all aspects of the running of the ship, not least the discipline of the officers and men, and directed the ship's course and conduct during battle.

Commodore

The rank of commodore was rarely filled, for it was in fact an intermediary post occupied by a senior captain temporarily commanding a small squadron or an important position on shore in the absence of an admiral. Specifically, the rank of commodore existed to satisfy the requirement of assigning part of a fleet to a senior captain while the admiral was commanding the remainder of the fleet on another assignment, or where the admiral was absent from the fleet altogether. A commodore could command an inshore squadron or a small number of ships, usually frigates, detached from their parent fleet to conduct the blockade of an enemy port, or he might also be assigned a particular task of attacking an enemy squadron or bombarding a position on the coast. If, as was usually the case, the appointment of commodore was only temporary, upon the expiration of his tenure the captain would revert to his own rank.

Admiral

Those in command at the highest level, in the name of the Admiralty, were the admirals, who led squadrons of approximately ten or more ships, or two or three squadrons, which composed a fleet. These men, all with years of practical experience dating back to the time they joined the Navy as midshipmen, were promoted automatically by seniority from the rank of captain. By the time they reached this rank they had demonstrated thoroughly their abilities at seamanship and command. They were expected to have a good grasp of strategy and be relied upon to execute the Admiralty's orders with steadfastness and

The battle of Trafalgar, a victory so comprehensive as to confirm British naval supremacy for the next hundred years. (Philip Haythornthwaite)

intelligence, since poor communication and great distances would often require an admiral to use considerable discretion in the interpretation of his orders. The members of the Admiralty generally knew admirals personally, and therefore were confident in entrusting them with direct responsibility over large numbers of ships and men. Not all admirals were suited to fleet command. Some performed administrative tasks ashore, some commanded shore establishments, and others governed British colonies. Admirals could retain their positions and rank for life, and thus they could be quite old and inefficient. Some took voluntary retirement on a sizeable pension; others worked until infirmity or death. There was no shortage of men from which to choose admirals, and by 1807 there were over 150 of them, often known as flag officers.

Unsurprisingly, an admiral in charge of a fleet (normally comprising at least 20 ships of the line, plus ancillary vessels, especially frigates) had myriad responsibilities, as shown by Keith's orders of 1799, which included 15 clauses. He was instructed:

To correspond with the governors of Gibraltar and Minorca, and all British consuls in the Mediterranean;

To give every assistance to the governor of Gibraltar;

To appoint such of His Majesty's ships and vessels under your command to convoy the homeward bound trade, as are the least fit to remain abroad, as you shall judge sufficient for their protection;

To detain and keep under his command any ships sent out to him, except storeships, which were to be sent back when unloaded;

To send surgeon's mates to help in Gibraltar hospital if needed;

To have his ships apply for provisions at Gibraltar;

To notify the Admiralty of any store and provisions lacking;

If purchasing any ships and vessels, to get Admiralty permission, and to have them surveyed by the commissioners at Gibraltar;

To conform to the established rules and customs of the navy;

Not to appoint any victualling officers on shore, but to apply to the Admiralty for permission;

The battle of San Domingo, 6 February 1806. Fought off the east end of the island of Hispaniola, in the West Indies, where a squadron under Vice-Admiral Sir John Duckworth defeated his French counterpart, Admiral Leissègues, whose vessel was forced ashore. As the British commander later reported to the Admiralty: 'the French admiral, much shattered and completely beaten, hauled direct for the land, and, not being a mile off, at 20 minutes before noon ran on shore, his foremast then only standing, which fell directly on her striking.' (Stratford Archive)

To visit ships and muster men, and see that they were rated properly, and to look to the cleanliness and economy of ships under his command;
To have his ships refitted at Gibraltar and Minorca;
To order his captains to take good care of rigging, stores and so on;
Not to allow his ships to come home except in cases of necessity;
And to keep a journal, and send regular reports to the Admiralty.

Admirals were classified according to three divisions, each of which contained three ranks. In the wake of the Anglo-Dutch wars of the 17th century, the Navy was divided into three squadrons, with a single colour designated for each, based on seniority: red was the highest, followed by white and blue. This flag was flown at the ensign staff of each ship in the fleet, though it is important to note that the white ensign was later altered to include the red Cross of St George in order to distinguish it from the flag of Bourbon France, whose flag was also white (though all possibility of confusion ceased when from about 1795 the French began to fly the revolutionary Tricolour). Admirals, like the red, white and blue squadrons of the fleet, were themselves subdivided into individual ranks, the most senior rank being (full) admiral, followed by vice-admiral and rear-admiral.

An admiral senior enough to command an entire fleet rather than merely a squadron normally positioned his flagship at its centre, whereas a vice-admiral, serving as second in command, directed the activity of the van (the leading squadron of the fleet), with a rear-admiral, as his title implied, commanding the rear. The senior post in this hierarchy – Admiral of the Red – required an officer to rise nine places once he was promoted from captain or commodore. Thus, his long ascent, facilitated by the retirement and death of those senior to him, began as Rear-Admiral of the Blue, which was the lowest rank of the lowest squadron. This was modified in 1805 when the rank of Admiral of the Red was redesignated to fall between Admiral of the Fleet and Admiral of the White, thus requiring those seeking the highest position to ascend ten places on the ladder of promotion. The most senior position of all – Admiral of the Fleet – entitled the holder of that rank to fly the Union flag (or 'Jack') at the head of the main mast.

The ranking of admirals can thus be summarized as follows:

Admiral of the Fleet
Admiral of the Red (rank created after 1805)
Admiral of the White
Admiral of the Blue
Vice-Admiral of the Red
Vice-Admiral of the White
Vice-Admiral of the Blue
Rear-Admiral of the Red
Rear-Admiral of the White
Rear-Admiral of the Blue

Ratings

Ordinary seamen

Seamen were categorized as befitted their experience and ability, and were divided into three rates: ordinary seaman, able seaman and petty officers. These men generally worked aloft, maintaining the sails and all the lines that controlled them, splicing and knotting, handling the rigging and heaving the anchors. Each man would perform his duties on one of two or three ship's watches, and bore responsibilities connected with each mast. As

Richard, Earl Howe (1726–1799). Commander of the fleet on the North American station during the War of American Independence (1775–83), Howe was one of Britain's most accomplished naval commanders, finishing his career with his tactical victory over the French at the battle of the Glorious First of June in 1794. He provided assistance to his brother, Sir William Howe, commander of British forces in North America, between 1776 and 1778, before assuming command of the Channel Fleet, in which capacity he brought relief to the besieged British garrison at Gibraltar. At the Glorious First of June, Howe captured six French ships from the fleet under Admiral Villaret-Joyeuse, for which achievement he was promoted to full admiral. He retired in 1797, though he was held in such high esteem that the Spithead mutineers approached him with their petition for referral to the government. (Philip Haythornthwaite)

described earlier, topmen – the fittest and, often, the youngest and most agile men – worked in the highest yards where work was precarious but vital. Older, stronger seamen performed their duties amongst the lower yards and on the forecastle. Finally, those of the afterguard worked on the quarterdeck and around the mizzen mast. Once battle commenced, however, most of the men, whatever their usual station, would be required to work the guns. Thus, in the course of only a short period at sea the ratings acquired a host of skills that enabled them to work in various capacities aboard ship. Beneath the ratings were landsmen who possessed no skills in seamanship and therefore were used for their brute strength to haul on ropes, rotate captans, and perform other laborious tasks. They could potentially acquire skills in the rigging if the captain allowed them into the lower rigging, but for the most part they remained on deck.

Able seamen

An ordinary sailor could rise to able seaman, which depended on his ability in certain skills. According to the Admiralty:

> The letters A.B., which mean Able Seaman, are placed against the names of only those who are thorough-bred sailors, or who, in the sea phrase, can not only 'hand reef and steer', but are likewise capable of heaving the lead in the darkest night, as well as in the daytime; who can use the palm and needle of a sailmaker; and who are versed in every part of a ship's rigging, in the stowage of the hold, and in the exercise of the great guns … In these, and twenty other things which might be pointed out, he ought to be examined by the Boatswain and other officers before his rating of A.B. is fully established on the books.

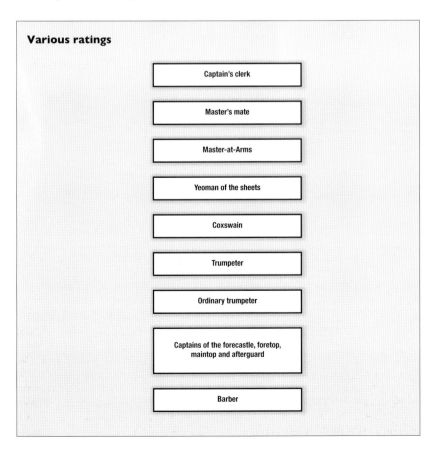

Various ratings

- Captain's clerk
- Master's mate
- Master-at-Arms
- Yeoman of the sheets
- Coxswain
- Trumpeter
- Ordinary trumpeter
- Captains of the forecastle, foretop, maintop and afterguard
- Barber

Examples of some of the many titles held by ordinary seamen aboard a British warship. In addition to his specialist skills, nearly every sailor understood the functions of the many miles of the ship's rigging and could find the correct line even in darkness or in the midst of a storm. He could tie perhaps two-dozen knots with ease, splice ropes in several ways and recognize the many hundreds of features aboard his vessel, from sails and spars to armament and equipment. If sent aloft, he could speedily make his way to the end of a yardarm to furl or reef a sail as required, applying his strength and dexterity under highly dangerous conditions.

Warrant officers

Warrant officers were men with specialist skills responsible for the maintenance and management of the ship. In contrast to officers of the wardroom who had become lieutenants with a commission granted by the Admiralty, the warrant officer received his commission independently from the Navy Board. Warrant officers had to be literate, as they were required to manage the ship's stores and keep an accurate account of them. They were subdivided into four categories, the first of which contained men enjoying the privileges of the wardroom and consisted of the master, surgeon, purser, chaplain and schoolmaster. The second category comprised the standing officers, being the boatswain, gunner and carpenter. The third section consisted of petty officers – the master-at-arms, sailmaker, armourer and carpenter's mate. Finally, belonging more properly to the lower deck, were the cook, caulker, ropemaker and sailmaker's mate.

The master was the most senior warrant officer, and was responsible to the captain for everything concerning navigation, steering and the general manner of sailing the ship. Thus, the master had charge of all navigational instruments, including charts, compasses, nautical tables and astronomical instruments. His additional duties required him to look after the condition of the rigging, sails, anchors and cables. It was his responsibility moreover to ensure that the ship sat evenly in the water, which meant that he had to supervise the stowage of provisions. Stores improperly loaded would adversely affect the ability of the ship to sail at its most efficient and could even imperil those aboard by causing the ship to heel. The master also maintained the security of the ship and had

Ropemaker's crew

Ropemaker

Sailmaker

Sailmaker's mate

Sailmaker's crew

These men made and repaired the miles of line that made up the ship's standing and running rigging. The sailmakers maintained and cut new sails, and repaired tears and holes created by high winds or enemy fire.

charge of the spirits aboard it, as well as the ship's logbook, or journal. It was this vital document that was produced at a court martial in the event the ship grounded, foundered or was otherwise lost. Masters often entered the Navy from the merchant marine, though others joined first as midshipmen or lieutenants, or had attained their rank by advancing up from quartermaster or as a mate from the lower deck.

Surgeon

The Surgeon was not trained by the Navy, but would have learned his profession as a civilian and then entered naval service after passing an exam at Surgeon's Hall in London or by a Physician of the Fleet if he applied for work while abroad. The Navy Board having granted him a warrant, he then served an apprenticeship as a surgeon's mate before receiving promotion to surgeon.

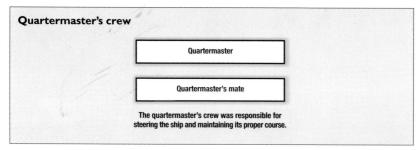

Quartermaster's crew

> Quartermaster

> Quartermaster's mate

The quartermaster's crew was responsible for
steering the ship and maintaining its proper course.

HMS *Sibylle* (38) in single combat with *La Chiffonne* (36) off Mahé, on the Indian coast. On 18 April 1801, discovering the French frigate anchored with a damaged foremast, Captain Charles Adam anchored 200yds from his opponent and began an action lasting 17 minutes, in the course of which the *Sibylle* received raking fire from a French battery positioned on the coast (left background). *La Chiffonne*, having suffered 53 killed and wounded, cut her cable, lowered her flag in token of surrender, and drifted on to a reef. Captain Adam, with only two men killed and one wounded, sent a boat to take possession of the prize and, turning his guns against the enemy battery, forced its surrender. As with most French vessels captured in serviceable condition, the Admiralty purchased *La Chiffonne* and commissioned her into the Royal Navy. (Stratford Archive)

Over 700 surgeons served in the Navy during the French Revolutionary and Napoleonic Wars. As to be expected, the surgeon was responsible for the health of the officers and crew, from administering the very crude forms of medicine of the time to those laid up ill, to coping with injuries from accidents, to performing operations, particularly in the wake of battle. He was also responsible for the management of the ship's sick berth, which stood on the orlop deck.

It was generally maintained that:

A naval surgeon of abilities and circumspection is generally the most independent officer in the ship, as his line of duty is unconnected with the others. He has the entire charge and management of the sick and hurt seamen on board his ship; is to perform surgical operations on the wounded as he may deem necessary to the safety of their lives; and to see that the medicines and necessaries with which he is supplied from the said board, or their agents, are in good in kind, and administered faithfully to the sick patients under his care.

Much has been said about surgeons being quacks or drunkards; clearly a few were incompetent or inebriated on duty, but most surgeons were well-intentioned and conscientious men with a good understanding of contemporary medical science (such as it was), who did their best under difficult circumstances.

Indeed, the difficulty of those circumstances is difficult to exaggerate. Surgeons had to cope with every conceivable malady and injury on a daily basis, including seasickness, abscesses, boils and toothache, to physical injuries – a common problem aboard ship with strenuous work so much a part of the regular routine – such as fractures caused by falls or concussion resulting from banging one's head on low deck beams or being struck by a falling object. The daily lifting and lowering of heavy objects like casks, barrels and boxes sometimes resulted in internal injuries and hernias.

Surgeons faced all manner of illnesses to try to prevent and treat, a problem exacerbated by the fact that contagious disease spread easily in an environment where all hands were confined to a small space. Thus, influenza, typhus and consumption (tuberculosis) could strike many members of the crew in a short period, while tropical diseases – malaria, cholera and yellow fever being the most common – found their way aboard, particularly among vessels operating in West Indian waters. Yellow fever was amongst the nastiest and most difficult diseases to treat.

On the rare occasions when men were allowed ashore, they sometimes returned with gonorrhoea and syphilis, and though scurvy had largely been eradicated by this time, it could occasionally crop up when supplies of fresh fruit and vegetables were exhausted and no rapid means of replenishing them existed. The resulting bleeding gums, listlessness and anaemia caused by the lack of vitamins became a daunting challenge to a surgeon for whom the necessary medications and citrus juices were unavailable.

Infection was one of the most common causes of death, whether from simple cuts or bullet or splinter wounds, the latter of which required either probing for the foreign object or amputation. If a limb were removed, the surgeon had to tie off the severed arteries and blood vessels with ligatures that were then left and allowed to fall off from the stump over time, thus leaving the exposed area at risk from infection. A sailor could endure a considerable amount of pain during the course of an operation – particularly in an age of regular hardship – but he still faced the great risk posed by post-operative infection, which, at its most extreme, could develop into gangrene or tetanus. Gangrenous tissue could be cut away during a subsequent operation, but lockjaw usually resulted from tetanus, from which recovery was rare.

During battle the most common injury was caused by flying splinters, showers of which were produced by shot striking and shattering wood planking, beams, stays and other features of the ship. A man hit by a ball itself might survive, though usually not without the loss of one extremity of another. In the midst of battle surgeons attended patients in the order in which they fell, irrespective of rank or severity of injury; triage did not yet exist. Amputation was commonplace and was carried out in a matter of minutes, not simply because of the urgency of other cases, but owing to the absence of anything like modern anaesthesia. A blow to the head or abdomen from a round shot usually spelled instant death, and there were many recorded instances of men being decapitated, though injuries of various kinds always outnumbered deaths. Surgeons also had to tend

Estimated number of fatal casualties in the Royal Navy, 1793–1815

Cause of death	Number	Percentage
Individual, non-combat (illness and personal accident)	84,440	81.5
Collective, non-combat (foundering, shipwreck, fire, etc.)	12,680	12.2
Enemy action	6,540	6.3
Total	**103,660**	**100**

to men who received burns from the discharge of the guns or from fire; fever and shock often followed such traumas to the body. Perhaps the most unlikely form of death connected with combat was what contemporaries called 'wind of ball', which meant the internal injuries caused by the flight of a round shot in close proximity to the victim's body. No outward signs of wounds were produced by this phenomenon, but there are a number of documented instances of passing shot, speeding past a seamen, causing instant death, though the victim was sometimes spared when the projectile passed his head rather than his abdomen.

Purser

The purser served in a civilian capacity in charge of managing the provisions aboard ship. As such, he procured all the food, spirits, wine, clothing, tobacco, bedding and other provisions needed for the entire ship's company. He actually ran a business of sorts, for while the Navy provided these various commodities, the purser was required to purchase some of these items with his own means and sell them on to the crew either for a profit in the case of clothing, or slightly underweight, in the case of food, profiting from the difference. Thus, for every pound of food supplied to the ship, the purser issued 14 ounces. When he sold clothing or tobacco he took a commission of five per cent and ten per cent, respectively. He also managed the distribution of coal and wood for the galley fire, the heating stoves of the officers' cabins and the lower decks, as well as lanterns, candles, wooden cutlery and other items.

The death of Lieutenant Grant at Copenhagen – a heavily sanitized version of the actual event, in which a round shot carried away Grant's head. The deck would also have been strewn with torn canvas, spent ammunition, severed lines, splinted wood, fallen men and pools or rivulets of blood, depending on the roll of the ship. (Philip Haythornthwaite)

Chaplain

The chaplain held the same rank as the master and surgeon, though obviously his position was not so essential to the daily routine of the ship. As a result, very few could be found aboard ships lower than third rates. Chaplains during this period were in all cases Anglicans, with responsibility for conducting religious services every Sunday for the entire ship's company, irrespective of the denominations actually represented. They were always in attendance at funeral services, which in almost all cases concluded with burial at sea, and held services of thanksgiving after battle. Chaplains were often learned men with training in theology, classical languages and modern languages – these last skills being useful in interpreting captured or intercepted dispatches and in communication with foreign ships and ports.

Schoolmaster

The schoolmaster, normally only found on a ship of the line, was principally concerned with the education of midshipmen in mathematics, theoretical navigation and trigonometry in order to prepare them for commissioning. Candidates for schoolmaster underwent an examination to ensure their fitness for the post. They might also teach reading and writing to the younger members of the crew.

Boatswain

The boatswain held many responsibilities and was answerable to the ship's master for all matters connected with the rigging, sails, cordage, blocks, anchors,

Admiral Cuthbert Collingwood (1750–1810). Collingwood commanded the *Barfleur* (98) at the battle of the Glorious First of June in 1794, but later transferred to various other ships, eventually becoming captain of the *Excellent* (74), then serving in the Mediterranean. In 1797 he distinguished himself at the battle of St Vincent where he captured two Spanish ships. Thereafter Collingwood took part in the blockade of Cadiz, becoming a rear-admiral in 1799 and transferring to the Channel Fleet, which blockaded Brest. Promoted to vice-admiral in April 1804, he commanded a squadron that joined Nelson off the Spanish coast in the autumn of 1805. At the battle of Trafalgar Collingwood, second in command, led the lee column and succeeded to commander-in-chief of the Mediterranean Fleet on Nelson's death. Collingwood continued to serve in the Mediterranean until he succumbed to exhaustion and died in 1810. (Philip Haythornthwaite)

cables and ship's boats. The boatswain was greatly experienced in all aspects of seamanship, and held the rank of a standing officer, which meant that he remained aboard the ship even when it was laid up and out of service. This ensured that when the ship was recommissioned, the same boatswain bridged the transition, for his intimate knowledge of the ship was invaluable to the captain. The boatswain not only inspected the rigging every day, but saw that his mates (all petty officers) roused the men to take up their watch on deck or aloft. Regulations required that he be:

> Very frequently upon deck in the day, and at all times both day and night, when any duty shall require all hands being employed. He is, with his mates, to see that the men go quickly on deck when called, and that, when there, they perform their duty with alacrity and without noise and confusion.

Responsible for the sails and a large amount of stores and equipment, the boatswain was required to provide monthly accounts to the captain indicating the articles purchased or used during that period. To prevent fraud, the ship's provisions were gathered and inspected by boatswains from other ships, and the boatswain would in turn perform the same service aboard other vessels. Prominent among his responsibilities was ensuring that the sails were kept in good condition and properly aired and dried. The boatswain saw to it that all the stores were removed and stowed ashore during re-fitting or when the ship was laid on its side and cleaned, a process known as 'careening'. Once the ship was ready for sea, the boatswain ensured that all the stores were returned aboard. While the ship sat at anchor, the boatswain saw that the sides were washed and kept free of lines or ropes.

Gunner

The gunner was responsible for the ship's ordnance, which meant more than merely the guns themselves, but also the magazines, gunpowder, shot, cartridges, gunlocks and other equipment such as small arms and edged weapons. The gunner remained with the ship when it was decommissioned, ensuring that it was ready for service at short notice. Together with the Inspector of Ordnance, who was dispatched by the Board of Ordnance, the gunner inspected all the guns and carriages supplied to the ship. He also checked to see that all magazines were dry and ready for the arrival of the

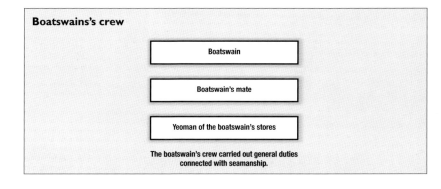

Boatswains's crew

Boatswain

Boatswain's mate

Yeoman of the boatswain's stores

The boatswain's crew carried out general duties connected with seamanship.

powder to be stored there. In addition to examining all the stores and equipment connected with gunnery, the gunner had charge over his mates, the quarter gunners, yeoman of the powder room and gun captains, and saw to the training of the gun crews.

As with the boatswain, the gunner was responsible for a large amount of stores and equipment, and thus had to provide accounts to the captain on a monthly basis showing the articles expended. In addition, he would account for the amount of powder, shot and small arms ammunition expended during practice firing. Again, like the boatswain, the gunner's stores were inspected by gunners from other ships to protect against fraud, and in turn he himself would be called upon to do the same aboard other ships. When the ship sat in dock for refitting or to be heeled over and its hull cleaned to remove barnacles and other sea creatures, the gunner saw that all the guns and associated stores were transferred to facilities in the dockyard. When the ship was ready again for sea, the equipment and guns were then re-embarked.

Carpenter

The carpenter had to serve a seven-year apprenticeship on shore before taking up his position aboard ship, which meant that he would have begun his trade as a civilian. He might then have spent another seven

years in the capacity of a carpenter or shipwright before joining the Navy. Many such men had worked in the Royal dockyards or in private facilities or been seized from merchant ships. The carpenter was responsible for a large quantity of supplies and equipment and therefore was accountable to the captain every month with lists showing the items expended in the course of his duty. He used specialist equipment, plus an array of other items such as nails, bolts, copper and lead sheeting, glue, glass, paint, pitch and tar. The nature of his trade also required that he managed a supply of timber to enable him to

British sailors and marines made numerous landings on enemy coastlines, either in support of the Army or to attain objects of naval significance. Landing parties carried out raids on docks, anchored naval vessels, fishing or merchant fleets, gun emplacements and arsenals in ports, and on fortified positions. Aboard ship, marines stood guard over the captain's cabin, the magazine and the ship's supply of alcohol, enforced discipline amongst the crew, lent their muscle for particularly arduous tasks such as raising the anchor, and sniped at the enemy during battle. (Philip Haythornthwaite)

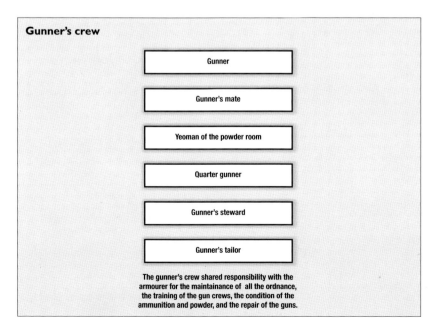

Gunner's crew

Gunner

Gunner's mate

Yeoman of the powder room

Quarter gunner

Gunner's steward

Gunner's tailor

The gunner's crew shared responsibility with the armourer for the maintainance of all the ordnance, the training of the gun crews, the condition of the ammunition and powder, and the repair of the guns.

Carronades in action. Gun crews varied in number depending on the size of the weapon: the heavier the ordnance the more men were required to handle it. These numbers fluctuated in any event, since some members of the crew might fall in battle or could be called away to perform another duty, such as taking part in a boarding party, working a pump when the ship sprang a leak or suffered an injury below the waterline, trimming the sails, or plugging a hole. Normally, the guns on one side of the ship remained unengaged, which meant that half the gun crews were theoretically available to assist their counterparts on the opposite side of the deck. In this case, the gun captain on the engaged side remained in command of his weapon, while his counterpart from across the deck became his second in command. (Angus Konstam)

repair the hull, as well as spare spars which lay in a crudely cut state to be prepared to the required specifications, whether for yards or topmasts, as circumstances demanded. The carpenter paid particular attention to masts that split as a result of heavy seas or high winds. In these cases, he attached a type of splint to reinforce them. As with the boatswain and gunner, the carpenter's stores were periodically checked to ensure that he was not engaged

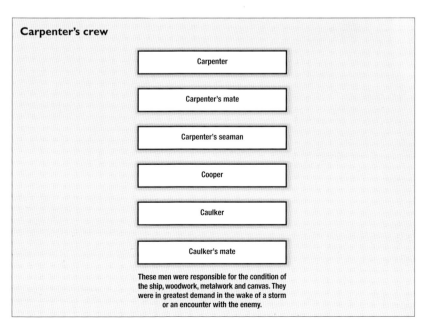

Carpenter's crew

Carpenter

Carpenter's mate

Carpenter's seaman

Cooper

Caulker

Caulker's mate

These men were responsible for the condition of the ship, woodwork, metalwork and canvas. They were in greatest demand in the wake of a storm or an encounter with the enemy.

in fraudulent activity. As the carpenter worked only during the day, he did not keep watches like most of the rest of the ship's company, and hence came under the category of 'idler'.

The carpenter was responsible, in addition to the aforementioned tasks, for determining if the hold contained any water that had leaked in, and if so to see that it was pumped overboard. He ensured that all the ship's pumps were in proper working order – a vital service, for without them the ship potentially stood in mortal danger. Water trapped in the bilge also had to be extracted, for it could have a deleterious effect on the health of the crew. The carpenter and the carpenter's crew played an important role in action, when they stood in the depths of the ship, below the waterline, ready to plug shot holes with oakum, nails, sheet lead and wooden plugs. When the ship was moored for refitting or careening, the carpenter would see that the hull was properly shored up by stout timbers, and that any newly fitted masts were firmly fixed at each deck level.

Armourer

The armourer worked with the gunner, looking after the small arms, both firearms and edged weapons, including muskets, pistols, cutlasses, pikes and tomahawks (sometimes called 'boarding axes'). In this respect he possessed skills as a blacksmith and understood and could repair the mechanisms and component parts of firearms. His task extended beyond weaponry to a limited extent, for he repaired anything aboard ship made of iron and could produce replacement articles such as nails, bolts and hinges. Often a civilian locksmith or blacksmith before entering naval service, the armourer repaired locks and any other device that required skills in metalwork.

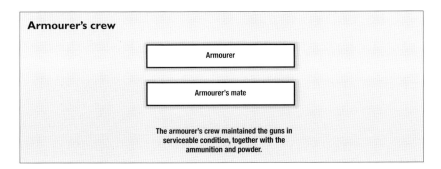

Armourer's crew

Armourer

Armourer's mate

The armourer's crew maintained the guns in serviceable condition, together with the ammunition and powder.

Cook

A ship's cook need not have any specialized skill in cooking, though he occasionally had civilian experience of working in a tavern. Occasionally the cook was a disabled sailor whose impairment fitted him for no other position aboard ship. The most junior of the warrant officers, the cook nevertheless held this position above the ordinary seamen as he had the important responsibility of maintaining the safety of the galley stove fire – the only major fire hazard aboard ship. In addition to preparing the ship's company's meals, the cook had to present clean utensils and pots for inspection every afternoon.

Ship losses through accident, 1793–1815				
Rating	Foundered	Shipwrecked	Burnt/exploded	Totals
Line (64 guns and over)	3	17	8	28
Frigates	4	67	2	73
Sloops, brigs, etc.	68	170	5	243

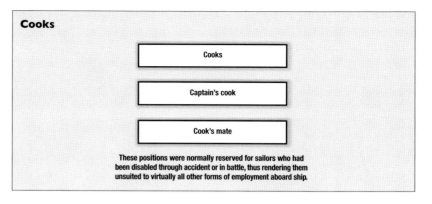

Cooks
Captain's cook
Cook's mate

These positions were normally reserved for sailors who had
been disabled through accident or in battle, thus rendering them
unsuited to virtually all other forms of employment aboard ship.

Marines

In addition to its ordinary crew, every warship from sloops through frigates and ships of the line was supplied with a contingent of marines, who comprised about a fifth of a ship's company. Approximately 120 marines served aboard a 74-gun ship, whose full complement numbered about 550. About 150 served aboard a first rate. Marines (who were designated 'Royal Marines' from April 1803) had originated as soldiers, drawn from foot regiments and assigned for service at sea. Unlike many sailors, marines were never pressed, but rather were composed entirely of volunteers who normally agreed to serve for the duration of the war. Many other differences separated sailors and marines, as one contemporary observer noted:

> No two races of men, I had well nigh said two animals, differ from one another more completely than the 'Jollies' and 'Johnnies'. The marines … enlisted for life, or for long periods as in the Regular Army, and, when not employed afloat, are kept in barracks, in such constant training, under

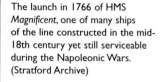

The launch in 1766 of HMS *Magnificent*, one of many ships of the line constructed in the mid-18th century yet still serviceable during the Napoleonic Wars. (Stratford Archive)

the direction of their officers, that they are never released for one moment of their lives from the influence of strict discipline and habitual obedience. The sailors, on the contrary, when their ship is paid off, are turned adrift, and so completely scattered abroad, that they generally lose … all they have learned of good order during the previous three or four years. Even when both parties are placed on board ship, and the general discipline maintained in its fullest operation, the influence of regular order and exact subordination is at least twice as great over the marines as it can ever be over the sailors.

When hostilities began in February 1793 the marines numbered only 5,000, but by 1802 they had expanded enormously to 30,000, a figure which remained about the same until fighting with France ended 12 years later. The Royal Marines were based at four locations: Chatham, Portsmouth, Plymouth and Woolwich.

Flogging. Discipline aboard ship was harsh, with sometimes dozens of lashes with a cat-o'-nine-tails administered for drunkenness, sleeping on duty, brawling and other infractions. Note the marines posted on the poop deck to ensure that the punishment is carried out without interference from the ship's company, the whole of which was required to observe proceedings. The accused is shown strapped to a grating awaiting his fate, while in the centre another sailor appears to be confessing to the crime in order to spare his (presumably innocent) comrade. Flanking the captain (left fore-ground) is the first lieutenant and two particularly young midshipmen. Two carronades, easily recognizable by their characteristic slide mountings and short barrels, may be seen on the ship's port side. (Stratford Archive)

Landing troops on shore. This was no easy matter, especially during a rough tide, as confirmed by one of thousands of British soldiers who disembarked in Mondego Bay, near Lisbon, in 1808: 'A rapid succession of these boats, closely packed with human beings, went tumbling through the surf, discharging on the beach their living cargoes, with little damage beyond a complete drenching. But as the day advanced, the surf increased, and each succeeding boat encountered increasing difficulties in reaching land'. (Philip Haythornthwaite)

Strength of Royal Marines, 1803–15												
1803	1804	1805	1806	1807	1808	1809	1810	1811	1812	1813	1814	1815
22,400	22,000	30,000	29,000	31,400	31,400	31,400	31,400	31,400	31,400	31,400	16,000	20,000

The Marines performed two functions: when at sea when their ship was not in the presence of an enemy they stood watch at various points in the ship such as at the admiral's and other officers' quarters, the magazine, the spirit room (where alcohol was stored) and other areas that required some form of security. In this capacity, marines served to prevent indiscipline and mutiny, and it is unsurprising that their own quarters, separate from those of the sailors, were strategically located near the wardroom, thus providing a buffer between the officers and seamen. When not acting as sentinels, marines assisted in various tasks, such as in adding their strength to those seamen engaged in heavy lifting and hoisting. Marines often assisted in hauling ropes, turning the capstan when raising the anchor to get under way, and carrying heavy loads. Marines were not required to work amongst the rigging, but might do so as volunteers keen to acquire the skills of an able seaman.

When their ship engaged the enemy, the marines' principal function was to provide small-arms fire, usually from the quarterdeck, when an opposing ship came within range of their muskets. They would also lead boarding parties or repel boarders on to their own vessel. Where their firepower and close-quarter fighting skills were not required, marines assisted at the guns, usually in some simple capacity that would enable them to leave this temporary post to assume their customary role elsewhere. During operations they provided a spearhead for soldiers or sailors, particularly against fortified positions and naval installations. Marines were also used in cutting-out operations, which involved seizing enemy vessels at anchor and either sailing them away as prizes or setting them alight. Marines could also be sent ashore to guard prisoners, weapons, powder or buildings.

British sailors and marines landing under fire at Aboukir Bay, on the coast of Egypt, 8 March 1801. (Philip Haythornthwaite)

Command, control and communications

Command and control

Perhaps surprisingly, instructions to commanders-in-chief were not issued upon appointment, but rather, in lieu of a new set of orders, the new commander inherited the standing or unexecuted orders of his predecessor. Even then, he received little in the way of guidance, such that he regularly made decisions without regular communication with the Admiralty. This was natural, particularly for commanders in distant stations such as in the West Indies, the Indian Ocean and the Mediterranean. Instructions normally came in the form of individual dispatches. A station commander was expected to maintain a regular correspondence with the governors of British colonies in his area, overseas bases and army officers, consuls and diplomats ashore; to make decisions regarding convoy duty in his area of operations; ensure the proper supply of his fleet; detach squadrons or individual ships as needed to perform special tasks; to keep in regular contact with his squadron commanders and individual ship's captains; to ensure the cleanliness and efficiency of the fleet; to arrange for ships to be refitted as necessary; to ensure that captains maintained the rigging, hull and stores of their ships in accordance with Admiralty regulations; and to send regular reports to the Admiralty on the affairs of his fleet.

Junior (vice- and rear-) admirals appointed senior captains to lead squadrons, particularly those composed of frigates. If, as it usually did, the fleet operated as a single cohesive force, junior admirals led divisions and squadrons within those divisions. A junior admiral led his division into action and saw that the individual ships in his division followed the orders of the commander-in-chief. The most senior of these men would also succeed the commander-in-chief in case of the latter's death. A junior admiral might also command a detached squadron, such as Nelson did in 1798 when he was sent by his senior, Lord St Vincent, to pursue the French fleet which had left Toulon for an unknown destination – which in the event proved to be Egypt.

Beneath the admirals were the individual ships' captains, who were responsible for the running of their ship. These men issued commands to their lieutenants who in turn executed them or passed them down to the midshipmen. The authority of the captain rested on more than his commission – and the fact that he could run his ship almost entirely as he saw fit – but on a combination of reward, punishment, courage, personal example and financial incentive. Thus, the captain possessed the power to promote on the spot anyone below the rank of midshipman and, indeed, often did in the wake of an action in which particular men had distinguished themselves. Punishments came in many forms, from 'disrating' (i.e. a demotion in rank) to the stopping of grog (the traditional sailor's drink), to flogging, with a dozen lashes being the maximum allowed without recourse to a court martial. In practice, however, a captain need only charge the offender with several offences and tally up the lashes awarded. The most serious offences were referred to a court martial, which consisted of between five and 13 members, all officers. Large numbers of lashes could be ordered for those found guilty, or even hanging. Captains also depended on prize money to encourage their crews. A condemned prize could be sold to the Admiralty, with the proceeds

Earl Spencer, First Lord of the Admiralty, 1794–1801. The period of his tenure proved a remarkably successful one for the Royal Navy, which during these years seized nearly all of the French colonial possessions in the West Indies, decisively defeated the enemy's Mediterranean Fleet, and generally drubbed it in all manner of engagements from ship-to-ship encounters to massive fleet actions. (Philip Haythornthwaite)

allocated to the captors according to a man's rank. Up to 1808 the captain was entitled to three-eighths of the prize money, with commissioned officers receiving one-eighth, warrant officers one-eighth, petty officers one-eighth, and the remainder of the crew, including marines, receiving one-fourth of the money paid for the prize. A new division of the spoils took effect from 1808

Management and administration in London
Government and Parliament
As Britain was a constitutional monarchy, the king, George III, did not exercise absolute power and relied on the prime minister and cabinet to make executive decisions, to which he almost invariably gave his consent, and to Parliament for the passage of laws and the allocation of funds for the running of the affairs of state.

With respect to the management of the Navy, the cabinet contained the First Lord of the Admiralty, whose decisions were subject to a consensus reached in cabinet meetings. Once a decision was made, the Navy depended on the House of Commons to vote it funds. The Commons, and to an extent, the House of Lords, took an active interest in naval affairs and regularly debated issues connected with the cost of the service and its role in the war. Above all, it voted the annual estimates that supplied it with money. The naval estimates were divided into three categories. The 'ordinary' funds covered the cost of maintaining ships and dockyard facilities. During peacetime these costs were generally higher, for during wartime much of the burden of maintenance was paid for under other categories. The second estimate was known as the 'extra', which were funds allocated for the construction of new ships. Lastly, Parliament conducted a vote to cover the cost of a particular number of seamen and marines, which largely determined the naval force available for that year.

The British Army was small as compared with Continental powers; the Royal Navy, on the other hand, exceeded 100,000 men and over 100 ships of the line, and had no comparable rival in the world, including France. Having said this, there were few checks to ensure that the money was used as intended, the number of men actually on service never quite reached the figures that Parliament pledged to fund, and there were no mechanisms to ensure that the money voted actually reached Navy coffers. More importantly, the money was never sufficient, so from year to year the Navy was chronically in debt. Contractors largely accepted this system, as payment eventually did reach them, so the Navy managed well enough from year to year, notwithstanding the fact that seamen's pay could fall into arrears for years at a time.

Naval expenditure, 1793–1802				
Year	'Extra'	'Ordinary'	Number of seamen and marines	Total naval supplies granted
1793	£387,710	£669,205	45,000	£4,003,984
1794	£547,310	£558,021	85,000	£5,525,331
1795	£525,840	£589,683	100,000	£6,315,523
1796	£708,400	£624,152	110,000	£7,613,552
1797	£768,100	£653,573	120,000	£13,133,673
1798	£639,530	£689,858	120,000	£13,449,388
1799	£693,750	£1,119,063	120,000	£13,654,013
1800	£772,140	£1,169,439	120,000	£13,619,079
1801	£933,900	£1,269,918	135,000	£16,577,037
1802	£773,500	£1,365,524	130,000	£11,833,570

Structure of naval administration, c. 1800

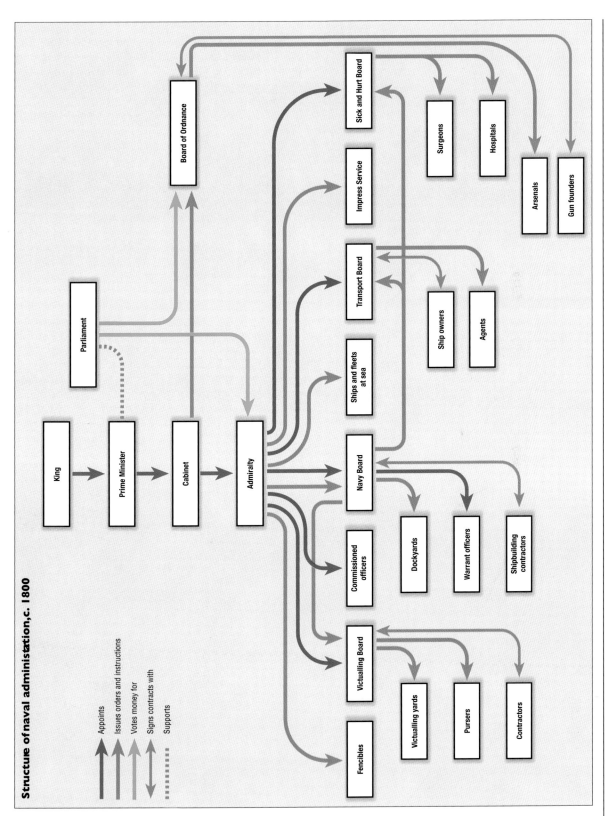

Quite apart from the officers and sailors who manned the various fleets, the Navy required thousands of government officials, clerks, labourers, inspectors and others to support it. In terms of cost, technological sophistication and complexity, no other institution in the world could match it.

The Admiralty

Responsibility for organizing the Royal Navy, planning and implementing its strategy and deploying its fleets and squadrons fell to, by modern standards, a remarkably small number of men at the Admiralty, who were responsible to the government. These seven men, the Lords Commissioners of the Admiralty, were not necessarily peers – indeed were often admirals – and answered to the First Lord of the Admiralty, who sat in the cabinet. As naval affairs were of such immense importance to the security of the nation, the Admiralty Board met on a daily basis in its offices in Whitehall, London, and determined the movement of ships as close as the Channel or as far away as the Indian Ocean and the Pacific. Supported by a working staff of 50 to 60, supervised by the First and Second Secretaries, the Admiralty performed various administrative functions, and saw to the commissioning and promotion of officers. These men exercised central control over the whole of the Navy, from determining the price the Navy would offer suppliers for food to deciding issues of great import such as the destination of a fleet in order to make contact with the enemy. Just as they exercised total control over the Navy, they also bore the burden of immense responsibility, for if through poor decision-making they contributed to major defeat, the security of the nation itself could be at stake.

At the time, the Royal Navy was the most complex and expensive institution not merely in Britain, but in the world, and its dockyards represented the largest industrial undertakings anywhere. From London the Admiralty executed the government's instructions, major and minor, relaying orders by courier to the relevant ports, or using the telegraph system which, from 1796, connected London to Portsmouth, Chatham and Sheerness, and later to Deal. From 1806 a connection existed to Plymouth, and two years later to Yarmouth.

Employment at the Admiralty Office was much sought after, for it was well paid and clerks and officers often served for decades, with promotion available for those who acquired the requisite experience and demonstrated a high capacity for efficiency. Within the Office were four subsidiary boards: the Sick

Expenditure on the Royal Navy, 1803–15				
Year	'Extra'	'Ordinary'	Number of seamen and marines	Total naval supplies granted
1803	£901,140	£1,488,238	100,000	£10,211,378
1804	£948,520	£1,345,670	100,000	£12,350,606
1805	£1,553,690	£1,394,940	120,000	£15,035,630
1806	£1,980,830	£1,435,353	120,000	£18,864,341
1807	£2,134,903	£1,557,934	130,000	£17,400,337
1808	£2,351,188	£1,142,959	130,000	£18,087,547
1809	£2,296,030	£1,408,437	130,000	£19,578,467
1810	£1,841,107	£1,511,075	145,000	£18,975,120
1811	£2,046,200	£1,578,113	145,000	£19,822,000
1812	£1,696,621	£1,447,125	145,000	£19,305,759
1813	£2,822,031	£1,700,135	140,000	£20,096,709
1814	£2,086,274	£1,730,840	117,400	£19,312,070
1815	£2,116,710	£2,278,929	90,000	£19,032,700

List of active ships, 1803–15 – the French Napoleonic Wars

Class	1803	1804	1805	1806	1807	1808	1809	1810	1811	1812	1813	1814	1815
First rates	6	6	7	7	6	6	6	6	7	7	7	7	8
Second rates	15	15	14	15	15	11	12	11	12	10	9	8	7
Third rates	90	94	95	98	102	109	109	107	105	103	108	103	94
Total ships of the line	**111**	**115**	**116**	**120**	**123**	**126**	**127**	**124**	**124**	**120**	**124**	**118**	**109**
Fourth rates	11	10	13	13	10	10	8	7	6	5	3	10	9
Fifth rates	102	106	114	125	138	141	144	146	139	137	123	134	126
Sixth rates	22	22	25	26	29	32	28	24	20	18	19	29	42
Sloops	78	91	121	131	172	191	251	246	225	209	214	212	185
Bombs	10	17	17	15	12	10	10	8	5	7	6	8	9
Fireships	2	2	1	0	0	0	0	0	0	0	0	0	0
Brigs, cutters, etc.	52	60	127	160	173	163	160	144	138	127	121	126	74
Grand total	**388**	**423**	**534**	**590**	**657**	**673**	**728**	**699**	**657**	**623**	**610**	**637**	**554**

First Lords of the Admiralty, 1793–1815

16 July 1788	John Pitt, Earl of Chatham
19 December 1794	George Spencer, Earl Spencer
19 February 1801	John Jervis, Earl of St Vincent*
15 May 1804	Henry Dundas, Viscount Melville
2 May 1805	Charles Middleton, Lord Barham*
10 February 1806	Charles Grey, Viscount Howick (Earl Grey, 1807)
29 September 1806	Thomas Grenville
6 April 1807	Henry Phipps, Lord Mulgrave
4 May 1810	Charles Yorke
25 March 1812	Robert Dundas, Viscount Melville (until 1827)

* admirals

and Hurt Board, the Transport Board, and the Victualling Board, all of which were responsible to the Navy Board. The Admiralty was also responsible for the Royal Marines, the Fencibles (a type of seafaring militia) and the Impress Service (which, in all but name, kidnapped or otherwise compelled men into naval service), as well as for operating intelligence services.

Each year the Admiralty commissioned ships with the funds provided for it by Parliament. The Admiralty was responsible for determining the basic specifications of a vessel before work began, with details provided respecting tonnage, dimensions, and the numbers and calibres of guns on each deck. Once these were laid down, the Surveyors of the Navy, employed in the Navy Board, would design the vessels on paper, to include details of the decks, hatchways, masts and other significant parts of the ship. Beyond this, the more intricate details such as the fitting and decorations were usually left to those at the dockyards themselves, where vessels were constructed either by workers at a government-maintained establishment, or by a civilian enterprise.

Admiralty Board Room. Decisions connected with the deployment of the Navy's ships and their operations were made here by a handful of senior naval officers and civilians. Note the maps rolled up and mounted above the fireplace. (Royal Naval Museum)

The Admiralty, the branch of government responsible for most of the administration connected with the nation's senior service and for the formulation and implementation of naval strategy. (Author's collection)

The Navy Board

The Navy Board, also responsible to the Admiralty, had to produce and deliver all the other needs of the Navy. This responsibility involved ensuring that ships were constructed, repaired and supplied with stores and equipment. The Board also controlled all the government's shipyards. Much of its work was contracted out to civilian companies which themselves employed a civilian workforce, and thus the Navy Board was sometimes thought of as the civilian branch of the Navy. The Navy Board had to ensure that the ships were adequately manned, and it was to it that fell the unpleasant task of gathering crews for the always expanding fleets and paying the men their wages. The offices of the Navy Board stored thousands of documents including contracts, lists, reports and letters, all filed and maintained by hundreds of officials and clerks, supported outside London by inspectors.

The Navy Board was responsible for building and supplying the ships and managing the dockyards, as well as the purchase and manufacture of all the equipment and stores required by the Navy. It also appointed most of the warrant officers, many of whom it examined. This whole enterprise involved thousands of men. The Board was virtually independent of the Admiralty and was the only one of the four boards that kept accounts. The Navy Board consisted of ten members, a combination of naval officers and civilians, whom the Admiralty Board usually appointed for life. A commissioner from each royal dockyard had a seat on the Board, the whole institution led by the Controller of the Navy, who was invariably a senior officer. While the Admiralty commissioned ships, the Navy Board designed them, usually care of the Surveyors of the Navy and their assistants and draughtsmen. British ships were often copied from captured French vessels, whose designs were much admired and often considered superior to those of British ships. After the Navy Board and Admiralty approved a design, the draughts were copied for the shipyards. In cases where ships were built in private yards, the Navy Board had to seek out builders and negotiate the cost from various competing firms.

In the course of the wars the Navy Board built approximately 100 ships of the line and 700 smaller ships and craft, representing over half a million tonnes, plus other ships built overseas. The largest ships – the first and second rates – were constructed in the Royal dockyards, with the remainder built in private yards. The Board dispatched someone to monitor the construction of all the vessels, which were often built in various sites along the Thames. Shipbuilding required the skills of 11 types of trade, above all that of shipwrights who reached this senior position only after seven years of apprenticeship in design and construction. Building a ship was a major enterprise: six months were required to build a sloop, between two and three years for a two-decked ship, and several years for a three-decker. Even then, once it was ceremonially launched, a ship still required several months for the process of fitting it out, including the erection of masts and placement of rigging, sails, stores, guns and other *matériel*.

Three subsidiary boards worked under the Navy Board umbrella: the Victualling, Transport, and Sick and Hurt Boards, all of whose members were, like the Navy Board, appointed by the Admiralty. The Victualling Board supplied the Navy with food, drink and clothing, and appointed pursers to oversee the distribution of such articles aboard ship. It ran its own bakeries,

John Jervis, 1st Earl of St Vincent (1735–1823). When war broke out with France in February 1793, Jervis commanded a naval expedition to the West Indies, where his squadron took the French islands of Martinique and Guadeloupe in the spring of 1794. He was briefly commander-in-chief of the Mediterranean Fleet in 1795–96, but the conclusion of a Franco-Spanish alliance obliged the British to withdraw their ships to the safety of Gibraltar. In February 1797, Jervis stood off Cape St Vincent, on the coast of Spain to prevent French and Spanish ships from the Mediterranean linking up with those at Brest with the intention of supporting a French invasion of Britain. Jervis's victory over the Spanish on 14 February, aided by Nelson's extraordinary conduct, put an end to the threat of invasion and Jervis was raised to the peerage as the Earl of St Vincent. In 1800 he took command of the Channel Fleet, and kept a continuous watch over Brest. He was appointed First Lord of the Admiralty during Henry Addington's ministry between 1801 and 1804. Although dictatorial and harsh, St Vincent set high standards for discipline and contributed much to the organization of the Navy. (Philip Haythornthwaite)

slaughterhouses and breweries to meet the needs of the sailors, and had its own ships to convey provisions to the Board's naval facilities at Gibraltar and elsewhere. The Sick and Hurt Board conducted examinations for surgeons, supplied their equipment, and managed the Navy's hospitals. The Transport Board conveyed Army and Navy personnel aboard a combination of privately hired merchant vessels and Navy ships. The Transport Board was noted for its efficiency and ran between 40 and 50 storeships for the Navy alone, with many more used for the Army. In 1796 the task of managing prisoners of war passed into its hands from those of the Sick and Hurt Board.

The Board of Ordnance

The Board of Ordnance, a government department separate from the Admiralty and based in the Tower of London and at Woolwich, held responsibility for supplying all the Navy's (and Army's) armaments – everything from pistols and dirks to cannon. The Board ran the factories that manufactured powder and guns; it provided the transport to convey the munitions and arranged contracts for work through civilian firms. It also experimented with new types of guns and powders and made studies of existing weaponry. The Board of Ordnance not only maintained supplies, it also had responsibility for equipment already aboard vessels and in the dockyards. This meant liaising with ship's captains to determine the condition of every weapon on his ship and the amount of shot and powder used, both during practice and in action. Guns and powder captured from the enemy had to be logged by captains, with the list of items sent on to London.

Proper functioning of this organization would not have been possible without a large number of officials and clerks, and the offices of the Board of Ordnance were lined with pigeon holes and boxes containing information in the form of lists and correspondence received from ships around the world concerning all the ordnance aboard every ship in the Navy. Every captain was required to account for the expenditure of all ammunition and shot, barring which he received a reprimand from the Board, wherever in the world he might happen to be.

Royal Navy dockyards and bases

At the beginning of the wars Britain maintained six dockyards, all run by the Navy Board. By 1815 these had launched 41 ships of the line and 78 other ships. About 60 private yards constructed another 60 ships of the line and over 600 other ships, some produced according to Admiralty design, others of

The Royal Dockyard at Chatham, in Kent, which could cater for just about any ship's material needs. Vessels ordered by the Admiralty were constructed according to plans based on a scale of 1:48. The keel was laid first, with the stem and sternposts attached and the frames erected to define the shape of the hull. Before the sides were planked with oak the frame of the ship was shored up to keep it vertical, and left to stand to season, sometimes for more than a year. In the course of construction and fitting out, a 74 required approximately 100 tons of ironwork, 30 tons of copper bolts, 12 tons of oakum, 5 tons of pitch, 12 tons of tar to coat the hull, 12 tons of copper sheathing and 4½ tons of paint. (Philip Haythornthwaite)

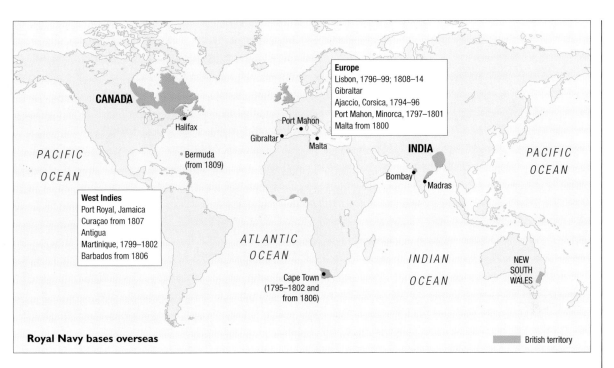

Europe
Lisbon, 1796–99; 1808–14
Gibraltar
Ajaccio, Corsica, 1794–96
Port Mahon, Minorca, 1797–1801
Malta from 1800

West Indies
Port Royal, Jamaica
Curaçao from 1807
Antigua
Martinique, 1799–1802
Barbados from 1806

CANADA

Halifax

Port Mahon

Gibraltar

Malta

INDIA

Bombay

Madras

Bermuda
(from 1809)

PACIFIC OCEAN

PACIFIC OCEAN

ATLANTIC OCEAN

INDIAN OCEAN

NEW SOUTH WALES

Cape Town
(1795–1802 and
from 1806)

Royal Navy bases overseas

British territory

the merchant yard's design with the intention of selling the vessels to the Admiralty. Private yards of course also produced merchant ships, some of which the Admiralty chose to buy and convert for its own needs. In addition to ship construction, the Royal yards also had to provide workmen for the Navy and repair and maintain its ships. Royal dockyards were situated at Portsmouth – the largest in the country – Plymouth and Chatham. A naval hospital stood at Haslar, near Portsmouth, together with an ordnance depot, a gunwharf and a marine barracks. Chatham and Plymouth had similar facilities. Portsmouth, Chatham, Sheerness and Plymouth were all fortified and were situated near the main anchorages. Ships in service only docked in port for refitting or to allow their crews leave; otherwise they remained at their respective anchorages, offshore, from where they could put to sea with little delay. Ships operating out of the Nore watched the Dutch coast; those in the Downs covered the North Sea and the southern coast of Holland; the anchorages at Spithead and St Helens were bases for ships monitoring the Channel; and Torbay served as the station from which to watch Brest, Spain and the Atlantic. Ships based at Plymouth operated in the Atlantic and beyond.

Dockyards in home ports could provide most of the needs of the Navy, but with its world-wide responsibilities the Royal Navy had to maintain bases across the globe. These facilities contained stores, food, depots for munitions, and equipment and materials for repairing ships afloat. In some cases medical care was provided, such as at Gibraltar. A civilian representative of the Navy Board oversaw the bases.

At the beginning of the wars in 1793 the Navy's overseas bases were located at Gibraltar, Halifax in Nova Scotia, and Jamaica and Antigua in the West Indies, but these were added to throughout the conflict so that by 1815 British ships could defend all the nation's principal trade routes. To supply the bases, the Admiralty bought naval stores in Britain and left their conveyance abroad to the ships of the Transport Board. The Victualling Board purchased food and drink for the use of the Navy, though supplies could be acquired locally when ships docked in foreign ports. As at home ports, the Board of Ordnance provided ordnance to British ports overseas, where ships repaired and replaced damaged weaponry.

The possession of these establishments across the world not only enabled Britain to protect her trade and colonies but to harass those of her enemies. The relatively small extent of the Empire at this period reveals that the great age of British imperial expansion – a prominent feature of the mid- to late-Victorian era – had not yet begun. British possessions on the Indian sub-continent in the early 19th century were still largely confined to Bengal, which, like Canada, had been conquered during the Seven Years' War (1756–63). Cape Colony, in southern Africa, was seized from the Dutch, a French ally, while New South Wales had been founded only a few years before the outbreak of war with France in 1793. Malta and Gibraltar, captured in 1800 and 1704 respectively, occupied key strategic positions in the western and central Mediterranean. Although extremely small in geographical terms, Britain's West Indian colonies remained her most valuable overseas possessions, with sugar, slaves and rum generating vast wealth for the Treasury.

HMS *St Albans* (64) being launched at Deptford, a private dockyard which supplied the needs of both the Navy and civilian commercial firms. Newly built ships in British yards were launched stern first, in contrast to vessels built on the Continent, and then towed away to be provided with masts and fittings elsewhere. The masts and yards for a third rate weighed about 70 tons, rigging and cordage a further 40 tons, cables and cordage about 44 tons, anchors 13 tons and sails eight tons. In addition to the various stores and equipment brought aboard a fully fitted ship, a 74 carried about 160 tons of ordnance, approximately 50 tons of ammunition and 350 barrels of powder. (Stratford Archive)

Various new ports were acquired during the course of the wars, two of the most important being in European waters. In the Mediterranean, the Army captured Minorca in 1798, thus enabling the Navy to use Port Mahon thereafter. When, however, peace with Spain was renewed in 1802 by the Treaty of Amiens, Britain restored the island to her erstwhile enemy. Port Mahon was of particular importance in enabling a fleet to watch the main French Mediterranean port at Toulon. Malta fell to British forces in 1800 after a two-year siege, providing the Navy with the invaluable port at Valetta, which was retained throughout the wars and formally acquired by Britain in 1814. The value of Malta as a base was recognized by many, including Admiral Lord Keith:

> Malta has the advantage over all the other ports ... that the whole harbour is covered by its wonderful fortifications, and that in the hands of Great Britain no enemy would presume to land upon it, because the number of men required to besiege it could not be maintained by the island ... At Malta all the arsenals, hospitals, storehouses, etc, are on a grand scale. The harbour has more room than Mahon and the entrance is considerably wider.

In North America, the Navy had use of Halifax and Bermuda, at the latter of which construction of a dockyard began in 1809. Britain also had temporary use of Alexandria, Egypt, in 1801–02, and Ajaccio, Corsica, from 1794 to 1796. Lisbon was available from 1808 to 1814 as a result of the British campaign in the Iberian Peninsula. In the Caribbean the Leeward Islands Squadron used the base at English Harbour, Antigua, while the Jamaica Squadron used Port Royal. Martinique was under British control from 1794 to 1802 (like other colonial possessions, returned to France at the Peace of Amiens), and Curaçao was taken from the Dutch in 1807. Ships operating as far as India made use of the base at Madras and the East India Company's dockyard at Bombay, which produced several ships purchased by the Royal Navy. In southern Africa, on the route to India, the Navy had access to Cape Colony with the fall of that Dutch colony to an expeditionary force in 1795. This was returned to Holland in 1802, but recaptured in 1806. One of the directors of the East India Company summed up the importance of this distant base:

> The importance of the Cape, with regard to ourselves consists more from the detriment which would result if it was in the hands of France, than any advantage we can possibly derive from it as a colony. It commands the passage to and from India as effectually as Gibraltar doth the Mediterranean; and it serves as a granary for the Isles of France; whilst it furnishes no produce whatsoever for Europe, and the expense of supporting the place must be considerable.

Communication at sea

Communication at sea proved one of the most difficult problems to overcome in the age of fighting sail. Admirals could speak face-to-face with their captains from time to time, particularly before battle if time permitted, and written orders could be sent to the various ships in the fleet by summoning boats to the flagship to collect such orders. If vessels passed close enough messages could even be passed vocally through a megaphone, though this was not always possible. In any event, such forms of communication were slow and altogether impossible during enemy action. The alternative was the use of flags. Prior to the new system developed at the turn of the 19th century, signalling flags had specific meanings. This served commanding officers reasonably well throughout the 18th century, but flags were limited in their application to particular circumstances, foreseen during peacetime, yet not always practical during wartime.

Admiral Lord Howe invented a system that employed 14 different flags, each of a different design, which was added to the Signal Book of 1790. These included ten flags representing the numbers one through nine, plus zero. Each numerical flag had a particular meaning, while four further flags were used to signify 'substitute', 'preparative', 'finishing' and 'affirmative'. Howe's system could create approximately 260 messages, though over time these were expanded in number and the design of the flags improved.

The most effective system of signalling, however, was the product of Admiral Sir Home Popham, who realized that Howe's system remained of limited value. In 1800, employing the same flags as Howe had used, he developed a system that came into immediate use. Popham's system involved the use of a combination of flags to represent words and phrases that enabled captains and admirals to create thousands of words very rapidly. The main advantage, however, rested on the ability to expand the vocabulary for words not already represented by flags. Any word could be spelled out letter by letter by using a flag for each letter of the alphabet. So comprehensive was

Horatio, 1st Viscount Nelson (1758–1805). Britain's greatest admiral and perhaps the most accomplished naval commander of any era, Nelson typified the bold, resourceful, aggressive character of so many Royal Navy officers of the French Revolutionary and Napoleonic era. When the war began in 1793, Nelson was captain of the 64-gun *Agamemnon* and served in the Mediterranean under Lord Hood. He first came to prominence in February 1797 when he demonstrated his daring at the battle of St Vincent by first cutting the Spanish line and then boarding two ships in rapid succession. He was badly wounded in a failed attack on Tenerife later that year, but his injury did not prevent him from further service, and he rejoined the Mediterranean Fleet in the *Vanguard* (74). In 1798 Nelson utterly crushed the French at the battle of the Nile, bringing an end to Bonaparte's dreams of an empire in the East. In April 1801 Nelson led the successful though costly attack against the Danish fleet at Copenhagen, adding further laurels to his reputation. The climax of his career proved, however, to be his apotheosis: victory over the combined Franco-Spanish fleet at Trafalgar on 21 October 1805 ended all realistic prospect of an invasion of the British Isles for the remainder of the Napoleonic Wars, but it cost Nelson his life. (Royal Naval Museum)

The battle of Copenhagen, 2 April 1801, an extremely hard-fought action in which the North Sea Fleet fought a formidable combination of shore batteries and enemy ships of the line at anchor. (Philip Haythornthwaite)

Popham's system that when Nelson issued his famous signal, 'England expects that every man will do his duty', only the word 'duty' needed to be spelt out as individual letters.

In addition to their being used to pass the admiral's orders, flag signals were employed for various purposes, particularly for conveying intelligence. Frigates were so placed around a fleet as to be in position to relay messages from one ship to another, to observe the horizon, and provide the admiral with timely warning of an approaching enemy. This was all very well in practice, but in reality a captain or admiral still had to decide up which mast his signal was to be hoisted to enable the recipient to see it clearly, considering the fact that the ships' positions sometimes shifted owing to winds, currents, or the decisions of individual captains. Lookouts had to keep a keen eye out for signals, otherwise the sender had to fire a warning gun to attract their attention. At night, signals could be sent using a combination of guns, flares and lights, with approximately 70 messages available by these means. Of course, in the smoke of battle, in fog or where relaying frigates were not to hand, signals might go unseen or fail to be understood. In rare instances, signals were ignored, the most famous instance being when in 1801 Nelson chose to disregard Admiral Parker's signal to withdraw from action during the battle of Copenhagen. Placing the telescope up to his blind eye, Nelson declared to the officers around him: 'I have only one eye. I have a right to be blind sometimes. I really do not see the signal.'

As we have seen, Popham's signal system was successfully employed at Trafalgar, and was the means by which Nelson's famous signal was conveyed to the fleet, read in the following order:

Read down the mainmast
Read down the foremast
Read down the mizzen mast
Read down the peak, or gaff
Read down the starboard side of the mainmast
Read down the port side of the mainmast
Read down the starboard side of the foremast
Read down the port side of the foremast
Read down the starboard side of the mizzen mast
Read down the port side of the mizzen mast

Admiral Lord Hotham's action, 13 July 1795, off Hyères, near Toulon. In the course of watching Toulon with the Mediterranean Fleet, Hotham enjoyed only limited success, proving himself unable either to contain in port, or bring to battle in a decisive encounter, the French fleet. He managed to capture the *Alcide* (74), but shortly after she struck, this prize caught fire and blew up with the loss of her entire complement of 615 officers and men. (Stratford Archive)

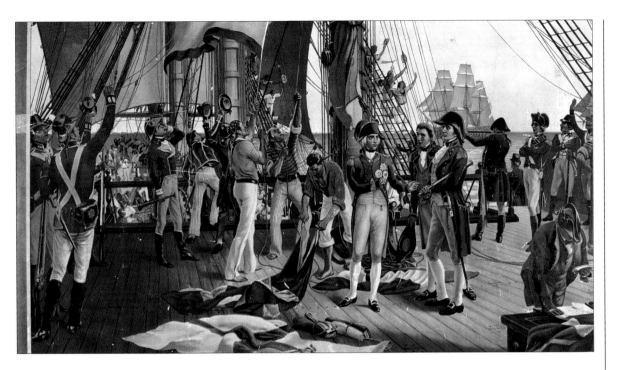

By interpreting the flags in the foregoing order, other ships could discern the message as follows:

Mainmast: '2', '5', '3': 'England'
Mainmast: '2', '6', '9': 'Expects'
Foremast: '8', '6', '3': 'That'
Foremast: '2', '6', '1': 'Every'
Mizzen mast: '4', '7', '1': 'Man'
Gaff: '9', '5', '8': 'Will'
Mainmast (starboard side): '2', '2', '0': 'Do'
Mainmast (port side): '3', '7', '0': 'His'
Foremast (starboard side): '4': 'D'
Foremast (port side): '2', '1': 'U''
Mizzen mast (starboard side): '1', '9': 'T'
Mizzen mast (port side): '2', '4': 'Y'

Nelson's famous signal at Trafalgar, 21 October 1805. (Royal Naval Museum)

As can be seen, however, the signalling system had its limitations; Nelson originally intended to say 'Nelson' rather than 'England' and 'confides' rather than 'expects', until his signalling officer, Lieutenant Pasco, observed that, as these words did not exist in the vocabulary, they would have to be spelled out, adding considerably to the number of flags required to make out the signal. Nelson readily agreed to the substitution, and the signal was duly transmitted with a manageable number of flags flying aloft.

Weapons and equipment

Ship types – rated vessels: ships of the line and frigates

Vessels of the Royal Navy were classified according to a system of 'ratings', based upon the number of guns they carried. A ship bearing 100 guns or more was classed as a first rate, a ship with 90 to 98 guns was a second rate, and so on down to 20 guns, which was classed as a sixth rate. Ships known as third rates and above qualified as 'ships of the line', while fifth and sixth rates were known as frigates. All of these vessels had three masts, the principal difference between them, apart from armament, being the number of gundecks. First and second rates had three, while third and fourth rates had two. All others had one deck. These differences may be summarized as follows:

Line of battle ships	
First rate	three gundecks, 100 guns or more
Second rate	three gundecks, 90–98 guns
Third rate	two gundecks, 64, 74 or 80 guns
Medium ships	
Fourth rate	two gundecks, 50–60 guns
Fifth rate (frigates)	one gundeck, 32–44 guns
Sixth rate (frigates)	one gundeck, 20–28 guns
Unrated	
Ship-sloops	one gundeck, up to 28 guns
Brig-sloops	one gundeck, up to 22 guns
Others	one gundeck, up to 18 guns

HMS *Victory*. A first rate mounting 100 guns on three decks and carrying a crew of over 800, she served as Nelson's flagship at Trafalgar. (Philip Haythornthwaite)

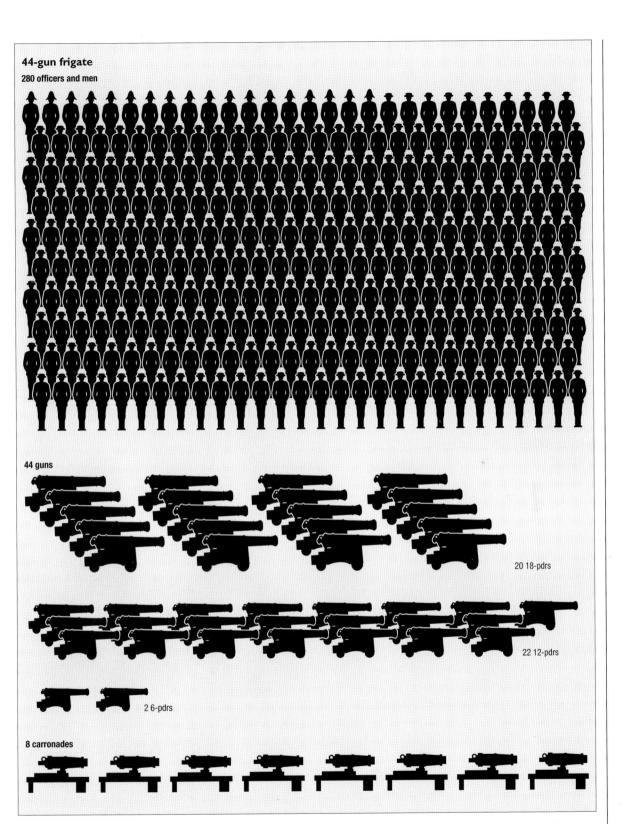

44-gun frigate
280 officers and men

44 guns

20 18-pdrs

22 12-pdrs

2 6-pdrs

8 carronades

A fifth rate ship, this heavy frigate carried various calibre guns mounted on a single deck. As frigates were too lightly armed and built to withstand the sort of punishment absorbed by two- and three-deckers in the line of battle, they instead served as fast cruisers operating independently of a fleet to patrol coastal waters, watch enemy ports, perform reconnaissance roles, or act as convoy escorts. Construction of a frigate of this size required over 80,000 cubic feet of timber from over 40 acres of woodland.

Typical ship statistics

Name	Launch	Length (ft in.)	Tons	Crew	Number of guns	Rate
Britannia	1762	178	2,065	850	100	First
Victory	1765	186	2,162	850	100	First
Hibernia	1804	201ft 2in.	2,499	850	110	First
Caledonia	1808	205	2,602	875	120	First
Boyne	1810	186	2,138	738	100	First
St George	1785	177ft 6in.	1,931	750	98	Second
Dreadnought	1797	185	2,110	750	98	Second
Africa	1781	159ft 6in.	1,379	500	64	Third
Stately	1784	160	1,376	500	64	Third
Bellona	1760	168	1,603	550	74	Third
Renown	1798	182	1,887	640	74	Third
Caesar	1793	181	1,991	650	80	Third
Endymion	1797	159ft 2in.	1,238	320	44	Fourth
Jupiter	1813	154	1,167	350	50	Fourth
Leander	1813	174	1,556	450	60	Fourth
Alarm	1758	125	679	220	32	Fifth
Apollo	1799	145	943	264	36	Fifth
Ariadne	1776	108	429	160	20	Sixth
Porcupine	1777	114ft 3in.	513	160	24	Sixth
Cormorant	1794	108ft 4in.	422	125	16	sloop
Bermuda	1806	107	399	121	18	sloop
Kangaroo	1795	95	313	121	16	brig
Cherokee	1808	90	235	75	10	brig

Three-deckers, which carried either 100, 112 or 120 guns, together with second rates, which had between 90 and 98 guns, acted as flagships and carried an admiral and his staff. These large vessels were not only expensive to build, but took years to construct and required very large crews, which accounts for the small number of the heaviest classes of ship.

Third rates carried either 80, 74 or 64 guns. The 74s were the most numerous of this type and were designed to fight an enemy vessel of any size. Ships bearing 80 or 64 guns were not as successful as the 74s and declined in number as the war continued. The 64s were less expensive to build than the others and were designed as line of battle ships, but as they carried 24-pdrs on the lower deck as opposed to the 32-pdrs mounted on the larger vessels, they fired a considerably weaker weight of broadside: 600lb compared to 800lb. Many such vessels were converted to store ships or harbour ships and seldom served with major fleets.

Ships carrying 50–60 guns were classed as fourth rates. These had two decks while fifth rates, most notably the 44-gun frigates, had one deck, as a

74s and ships of the line in commission

	1793	1796	1799	1801	1805	1808	1811	1814
74s	19	54	58	56	49	76	80	73
All ships of 64 guns or more	26	105	105	100	83	113	107	99

Classification of naval vessels, 1793–1815

Rating	Type of ship	Armament	Number of men	Rank of senior officer
First rates	Line of battle	100+ guns on three gundecks	841	Post captain
Second rates	Line of battle	90 to 98 guns on three gundecks	743	Post captain
Third rates	Line of battle	80, 74 or 64 guns on two gundecks	494–724	Post captain
Fourth rates	Below the line	50–60 guns on two gundecks	345	Post captain
Fifth rates	Frigates	32 to 44 guns on one gundeck	217–297	Post captain
Sixth rates	Frigates	20 to 28 guns on one gundeck	138–198	Post captain
Sloops	Unrated	up to 28 guns on one gundeck	121–135	Commander
Brigs	Unrated	up to 22 guns on one gundeck	80–121	Commander
Others	Unrated	up to 18 guns on one gundeck	varied	Lieutenant

Boat action. In 1800, Lieutenant Beaufort of the *Phaeton* led an attack against a Spanish poleacre moored in the harbour of Fuengirola: 'I went away with the pinnace, two five-oared cutters and the launch with carronade … At 3 o'clock, arrived in shore in smooth water, where I intended laying by a few minutes to rest the people's arms after so fatiguing a pull … But the alarm being given on the beach, and fires, muskets, etc, communicating our station to the ship, I had no time to hesitate but pushed on directly … When, within about two cutters' lengths, she fired a few shots but without other effect than as a signal for us to rush on and giving inspiring cheer, I soon found myself under the starboard main chains. She was soon carried as the officers and sailors had deserted the deck and nobody remained upon it but the marines, who indeed defended it bravely.' (Philip Haythornthwaite)

'Great' or 'long' gun. After this weapon was discharged, it recoiled inboard, with ropes restraining the ordnance to prevent it from moving out of control. The muzzle was then sponged out to render safe any unburnt fragments of the spent cartridge case or powder, which might otherwise set off a premature explosion when the next cartridge was rammed down the barrel. (Philip Haythornthwaite)

Alexander Hood, First Viscount Bridport (1726–1814). At the start of the French Revolutionary Wars Hood was appointed Admiral Lord Howe's second in command and served at the Glorious First of June in 1794, commanding the rear of the fleet and receiving a peerage for his conduct. At the battle of Ile de Groix on 23 June 1795 Hood captured three French ships, but was criticized for failing to inflict a decisive blow on the enemy. He was given command of the Channel Fleet in March 1797, just prior to the outbreak of the mutiny at Spithead. Hood failed to stem its spread to most of the fleet and eventually his flagship, too, refused to take orders from its officers. After the mutiny, which ended peacefully, he spent years blockading Brest before retiring after 60 years of naval service. (Philip Haythornthwaite)

consequence of which they did not possess the firepower or structure to be able to hold their place in the line of battle. Nor were fourth rates fast enough to serve as frigates, as a result of which this type of vessel also declined in number as the war progressed. Single-decked frigates, carrying between 28 and 44 guns, on the other hand, could manoeuvre well, were fast, and sufficiently well-armed to be able to perform operations independently of the fleet, or as part of an all-frigate squadron. If attached to a fleet, frigates performed reconnaissance duties for the commander-in-chief, with their main function being to locate the enemy fleet, notify the admiral of its location and course, and follow it until battle was joined. All navies respected the unwritten convention that a frigate was not to be fired upon by a ship of the line during fleet actions unless the frigate fired first.

The smallest of rated vessel was the sixth rate post-ship, the lighter of the two types of frigate, which carried 20 to 28 guns, making it slightly larger than a sloop. Beneath this came 'unrated' vessels, such as sloops, which were armed with up to 28 guns. Brigs and schooners fell below these, with gunboats smaller still.

When considering the number of guns associated with a ship, it is important to note that this unrefined statistic reveals less about the strength of a ship than appears obvious on the surface, for numbers of guns say nothing of the actual weight of shot they fired. Thus, the main armament of a 74 was the 32-pdr cannon (the weight, of course, referring to that of the shot, not the ordnance itself), while those on a 64 were 24-pdrs. Moreover, no ship mounted all the same type of guns. Thus, while a 64 self-evidently carried 64 guns, these were a mixture of 26 24-pdrs, the same number of 18-pdrs, and 12 12-pdrs. Finally, carronades were not counted when calculating armament, which meant that the fighting power of a ship, particularly at close range where carronades could inflict considerable damage, was not uniformly reflected in the tabulation of long guns (i.e. ordinary cannon) alone.

Ship types – unrated vessels

Sloops

This category covered a large variety of small vessels. Though less glamorous than the ships of the line that fought the main actions, or even the frigates, many of which fought celebrated ship-to-ship encounters, hundreds of small vessels enabled the Royal Navy to function. Tasks such as inshore patrols and convoy escort duty were vital, if tedious and repetitive, and kept Britain's naval war against France alive. The largest unrated vessel was the ship-sloop (usually abbreviated to 'sloop'), which came in several variations, but in all cases was smaller than a sixth rate frigate and was led by a commander instead of a post captain. Some sloops had both a quarterdeck and a forecastle, others had neither, with the upper deck running continuously the length of the vessel. Most sloops were two masted (thus qualifying them as 'boats' rather than as 'ships'), though they could occasionally appear in a three-masted version.

The tasks performed by sloops varied, but included the protection of commerce, inshore defensive patrols conducted all along the coasts of Britain and Ireland to protect against invasion and smuggling, and patrols designed to harass the enemy's coasts. The sloop could not perform the functions of a weakly armed frigate since its armament was insufficient for such duties and because it was quite slow, so that it suffered from the double disadvantage of being not only unable to outrun an enemy frigate but was also incapable of defending itself from one. Most sloops carried carronades that were ideal at short range. Sloops with three masts usually carried up to 28 guns on the upper deck as well as swivel guns on the quarterdeck and forecastle. These were gradually replaced by 32-pdr carronades on the upper deck and six 12-pdr carronades on the quarterdeck, plus two 6-pdr long guns as chasers. The Navy List in 1805 contained 39 vessels of this type, and 57 ten years later at war's end.

Brigs

Slightly smaller than the sloop and led by a lieutenant rather than a commander, the brig-sloop (or, more commonly, simply 'brig') usually carried 14 24-pdr carronades, but might also carry a number of long guns. Such vessels were sometimes converted merchantmen where shortages in the Navy could be made up. Two square-rigged masts propelled a brig.

Bomb vessels

These were shallow-draught vessels used to approach close in shore and fire shot by high trajectory into the interior of a fortification or town. Bomb vessels contained mortars mounted so as to be able to fire at a high angle. Seventeen such vessels were in commission in 1805, and were employed in the attack on Copenhagen in 1807, against Walcheren in 1809, and in the attack on Fort McHenry during the Anglo-American War of 1812.

Fireships

Fireships were loaded with combustibles and handled by a skeleton crew who would manoeuvre the vessel into a position from which it could be carried by the wind or current into an anchored enemy fleet. Just prior to releasing a fireship on its somewhat uncertain course, the crew would light the fuses to the explosive charges or inflammable material and make their escape in boats. A few purpose-built fireships existed in the Royal Navy during the wars, but they were generally fitted out only when a particular need arose, such as at Toulon in 1793 and during the attack on the Basque and Aix Roads in 1809. Employing fireships was particularly difficult, for they tended only to achieve success when sent against a large enemy fleet at anchor and amidst favourable wind and tide conditions – these last being particularly fickle.

Schooners

Schooners normally carried two masts, and were fast but weakly armed, with square topsails on the foremast and gaff-rigged courses aft. They were well suited for carrying messages between ships and in the pursuit of other, similarly armed and built enemy craft, such as privateers.

Gunboats

Gunboats were powered by oars or a single sail, and sometimes by both, and armed with one or two heavy guns at either end. Such weapons could only fire straight ahead, for the recoil would capsize the craft if the ordnance were placed in any other position. Gunboats served in harbours and inshore waters, but could not attack a larger vessel except when deployed in great numbers, such as on Lake Borgne in December 1814 during the campaign against New Orleans. Thus, a brig or sloop, if stationery owing to becalmed conditions, could occasionally fall prey to a swarm of gunboats, particularly if close to shore.

Ships' boats

While vessels lay in harbour their boats could carry people and stores between themselves and the shore, or between ships. Ships' boats could also patrol around the ship while it was anchored in a foreign port to prevent an enemy from approaching or to stop sailors from deserting. Boats could also aid in communication between ships at sea and rescue men who had fallen overboard. Most importantly, boats played an essential role in amphibious operations and cutting-out expeditions, which sometimes required lengthy bouts of rowing. Ships' boats could also be used to tow a damaged vessel or one stuck in a calm, or for moving the anchors. Boats were stowed on the parent vessel, but in battle were often towed astern to protect them – not always with success owing to stray shot – from enemy fire. If left aboard during an action, ships' boats were often riddled with musket balls and shattered by all manner

Cutting out of the *Chevette*, 21 July 1801. Moored in Cameret Bay, this French corvette was the target of boats sent by the frigates *Beaulieu* and *Doris*. The British failed to take her on the night of 20 July, but returned with reinforcements the following night and seized her. (Stratford Archive)

of projectile emerging from the guns, and thus rendered useless. Even if they remained intact, boats were not intended to be used as lifeboats, not least because they were not numerous enough to carry the entire crew.

Ordnance

Long guns and carronades

From the mid-16th century until the Napoleonic Wars the function and design of guns changed very little, with ordnance consisting of a simple metal tube down the muzzle of which was rammed a charge and round ball. The charge was then ignited by a fuse that communicated with the powder down a vent at the breech, at the top rear of the gun. In the 1780s foundries ceased to manufacture guns from brass and began to cast them in a far stronger and more reliable material, iron, which made it possible to produce guns as one solid piece which could then be bored out, thus creating stronger barrels less likely to explode. Naval ordnance was classified according to the weight of the round shot it fired. Thus, in straightforward fashion, an 18-pdr fired an 18lb ball. Frigates and ships of the line also carried 24-pdr and 36-pdr guns, with the heaviest ordnance always arrayed on the lowest gundeck to ensure the stability of the ship.

The battle of the Glorious First of June (1794), the first fleet action of the French Revolutionary Wars. Admiral Howe intended to break through the enemy's line and engage it to leeward, obliging the French to fight while preventing any damaged ships from escaping. In the event, some of his captains either misunderstand his order or deliberately disobeyed it, and only six ships executed the order as Howe intended it to be interpreted. After days of pursuit, Howe had finally closed with his opponent, but by failing to intercept the enemy grain convoy sailing under the protection of the fleet commanded by Admiral Villaret-Joyeuse, did not achieve the decisive engagement he sought. (Philip Haythornthwaite)

Weight of shot	Length of piece	Weight of piece	Weight of gun and carriage	Diameter of the shot	Average charge	Range: point blank	Range: maximum at 6 degrees	Number of crew
42-pdr	9ft 6in.	3.25 tons	3.90 tons	6.68in.	14.0lb	400yds	2,740yds	16
32-pdr	10ft 0in.	2.90 tons	3.47 tons	6.10in.	10.6lb	400yds	2,640yds	14
32-pdr	9ft 6in.	2.75 tons	3.27 tons	6.10in.	10.6lb	400yds	2,640yds	14
24-pdr	10ft 0in.	2.60 tons	3.09 tons	5.54in.	8.0lb	400yds	1,980yds	12
24-pdr	9ft 6in.	2.47 tons	2.95 tons	5.54in.	8.0lb	400yds	1,980yds	12
24-pdr	9ft 0in.	2.78 tons	2.85 tons	5.54in.	8.0lb	400yds	1,980yds	12
18-pdr	9ft 6in.	2.10 tons	2.52 tons	5.04in.	6.0lb	350yds	2,110yds	10
18-pdr	9ft 0in.	2.00 tons	2.40 tons	5.04in.	6.0lb	350yds	1950yds	10
12-pdr	9ft 0in.	1.60 tons	1.92 tons	4.40in.	4.0lb	375yds	1,320yds	10
12-pdr	8ft 6in.	1.57 tons	1.89 tons	4.40in.	4.0lb	375yds	1,320yds	10
12-pdr	8ft 0in.	1.46 tons	1.75 tons	4.40in.	4.0lb	375yds	1,320yds	10
9-pdr	7ft 6in.	1.23 tons	1.47 tons	4.00in.	3.0lb	330yds	1,730yds	8
9-pdr	7ft 0in.	1.15 tons	1.37 tons	4.00in.	3.0lb.	330yds	1,730yds	8
6-pdr	8ft 0in.	1.10 tons	1.32 tons	3.49in.	2.0lb	320yds	1,555yds	4
6-pdr	6ft 0in.	0.82 tons	0.99 tons	3.49in.	2.0lb	320yds	1,555yds	4
4-pdr	6ft 0in.	0.61 tons	0.73 tons	3.05in.	1.3lb	310yds	1,250yds	4
4-pdr	5ft 6in.	0.56 tons	0.67 tons	3.05in.	1.3lb	310yds	1,250yds	4
3-pdr	4ft 6in.	0.36 tons	0.44 tons	2.77in.	1.0lb	300yds	1,225yds	2 or 3

Specifications of standard carriage-mounted guns

The carronade was invented by General Robert Melville in 1752 at the Carron Iron Works and first manufactured for naval service in 1779. It had a shorter barrel than an ordinary 'long gun' and used a smaller powder charge to fire a heavy round shot, up to 64lb in weight. The carronade came into use in the Royal Navy during the War of American Independence (1775–83) and thereafter became standard on the quarterdecks of frigates and as the main armament of sloops and brigs. These weapons could produce a crushing broadside if fired at very close range, and their low velocity tended to produce great clouds of deadly splinters upon striking the enemy's hull, as opposed to penetrating it. The carronade was mounted on a slide rather than on a wheeled carriage and could fire case or grape shot as an anti-personnel weapon – highly effective in clearing the enemy deck.

Nevertheless, carronades were revealed to be something of a liability during the War of 1812 when, during ship-to-ship actions, American ships simply kept their distance and bombarded their British adversaries from a distance beyond the range of the carronade. In the last years of the Napoleonic Wars, therefore, carronades were withdrawn from newly built smaller ships and replaced by standard ordnance.

Chase guns, swivel guns and rockets
Considerably smaller in calibre than the carronade was the chase gun or 'chaser', mounted on the bow to fire forward from the forecastle, and hence the name 'bow-chasers', or alternatively mounted on the stern to fire from the poop or quarterdeck. These weapons fired a 6lb or 9lb shot, and were made of brass, a material which better suited small pieces of ordnance in terms of facilitating accuracy, whereas iron was reserved for standard ordnance.

Ranges of carronades in yards							
Weight of shot	Charge	Point blank	at 1 degree	at 2 degrees	at 3 degrees	at 4 degrees	at 5 degrees
12-pdr	16oz.	230	400	690	740	810	870
18-pdr	24oz.	270	470	730	800	870	1,000
24-pdr	32oz.	300	500	870	870	920	1,050
32-pdr	42oz.	330	560	830	900	970	1,087
42-pdr	56oz.	400	600	860	980	1,020	1,170
68-pdr	88oz.	450	650	890	1,000	1,000	1,280

Bow-chasers were employed to fire at a vessel being pursued, with the intention of striking its masts or rigging, disabling it sufficiently to prevent the vessel's escape. Stern-chasers were used against a pursuing ship, with the similar intention of disabling it sufficiently to bring an end to the chase.

Swivel guns constituted the smallest form of ordnance. These were mounted on swivels so that they could fire at practically any angle. Like chasers, these served as anti-personnel weapons, loaded with lead shot and fired at close range, particularly at enemy boarders. They were often mounted on the ship's rail, but they were small enough to be carried aloft before action and, together with a gun mount, lashed to a spar or top and used to fire down onto the enemy's deck. Swivel guns were also ideal weapons aboard ships' boats, particularly when employed against opposing boats.

Although rockets were invented centuries before in China, William Congreve, who worked at the Board of Ordnance, put them to effective military use in the West. The rocket which came to bear his name was little more than a rudimentary warhead in the form of a pointed metal cylinder filled with gunpowder, attached to a long stick to stabilize its flight. Warheads came in different varieties, depending on their purpose. Some were explosive for use against ships or troops ashore, while others were incendiary, to be used against ships, harbour facilities and coastal towns. Some contained shrapnel for use against enemy crews or formed units on shore. Rockets, like ordinary

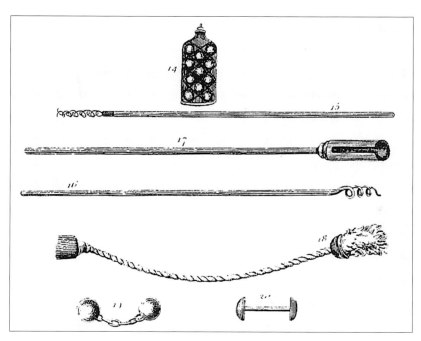

Gun tools and ammunition, showing, from top to bottom: case shot, a scouring worm, a ladle, a worm, a flexible rammer and sponge, chain shot and bar shot. (Angus Konstam)

ammunition, were classified according to their weight, with the 32-pdrs and 42-pdrs being the most common. The former had a range of 3,500 yards, but they and all other rockets were wildly inaccurate and could only be depended on to fall in the general area intended. The 32-pdr rocket was made of a 42in. iron cylinder, four inches in diameter, at the tip of which was fitted a conical nose. A 15ft stabilizing stick was attached to the side of the cylinder. Rockets were normally fired by small boats specially fitted for such weapons, including a frame mounted on the deck in such a way as to be unencumbered by sails or rigging. Thousands of rockets were used in 1807 to destructive effect during the bombardment of Copenhagen, much of which caught fire as a result.

Types of ammunition

Various types of ammunition were used by the Navy, the most common being a solid iron ball called a round shot (the term 'cannon ball' was not in use at the time and, indeed, is merely a landsman's term which was never applied to artillery, whether on land or at sea). Gun crews could also make use of a variety of anti-personnel ammunition, including canister shot, which consisted of a cluster of small shot held together in a canvas bag or thin metal container. They could also make use of langridge, which comprised scrap metal similarly held together so that on discharge the container easily broke open and spread its contents like a giant shotgun. Such ammunition was only effective at short range, but if fired at a crowded enemy deck when close at hand the results were devastating.

Other forms of ammunition were reserved for destroying enemy rigging or to damage, if not destroy, the enemy's masts. Chain shot, which consisted of two balls attached by metal links, could tangle or cut through lines and shred sails, thereby impeding the enemy's ability to control his direction and speed. Bar shot, which consisted of two spheres joined by an iron bar, performed a similar function, though it was more effective than chain shot against masts and spars. The Board of Ordnance specified the number of rounds to be carried for each gun when a ship left port. For a ship of the line this was typically 80 round shot, three of chain or bar shot, and five of canister shot.

Hot shot was a variation of ordinary round shot, which was heated to a critical redness in a special furnace before being loaded into a gun and fired at an opposing ship or some other target vulnerable to burning. Preparing hot shot was an exceedingly risky venture, for on a rolling ship the shot could fall from its special cradle and, in any event, finding a suitable and safe place for a furnace aboard ship was no easy matter. Hot shot therefore was principally the weapon of choice of shore batteries seeking to destroy enemy ships. Loading

Opposing crews come to grips in hand-to-hand fighting. (National Maritime Museum, neg. x164)

The battle of St Vincent,
14 February 1797, where Nelson,
though not in command, broke the
Spanish line on his own initiative.
(Philip Haythornthwaite)

this glowing red ammunition required special care: two men carried it in special tongs to the gun, which had been prepared with a charge protected by a damp wad, or wet clay, before being rammed home. Without this precaution, the heat of the shot could cause a premature explosion, wasting the ammunition and perhaps injuring some of the gun crew in the process. Time was also of the essence, for the crew had to act swiftly by ramming a second wad in front of the shot before training the gun and firing it.

To propel these various types of ammunition, ships carried vast amounts of gunpowder, stored in the magazine. Gunpowder, properly known to contemporaries as 'black powder', was produced from a composite of saltpetre (potassium nitrate), sulphur and fine charcoal. A process known as 'corning' converted these substances into granules of varying degrees of fineness. The largest guns used the coarsest variety, while small hand-held firearms like pistols required the finest type, which was also used in priming the charges of cannon. Members of the crew made up charges for the guns in the form of cartridges, consisting of flannel or paper containers of varying sizes, depending on the weight of powder required. Naturally, the heavier the ammunition, the greater the weight of charge needed to propel it. A full charge for a 32-pdr, for instance, required 11lb of powder. To issue a salute, which of course required no ammunition at all, only 6lb were needed.

As black powder is highly combustible, nothing more than a simple spark is required to detonate it. It therefore required special handling and was carefully stored in a magazine, or 'powder room', situated deep within the ship, far from the galley and other sources of fire or sparks. As it became useless when wet, the powder also had to be protected from water. Magazines were situated next to the 'filling room' where cartridges were prepared. The use of iron tools and equipment in or near the magazine was strictly forbidden, notwithstanding the fact that the powder was stored in wooden barrels, ostensibly proof from danger. Even the barrels were bound with copper or wooden hoops, rather than the standard iron ones, to reduce the risk of catastrophe. Such was the volatility of black powder that a fire in the magazine, whether from a candle, spark, flame or enemy shot, nearly always resulted in the instantaneous destruction of the ship.

Black powder was a crude substance which when fired produced a dense cloud of white smoke which, in the absence of wind, could remain in place for several minutes, reducing visibility for the gunners and obscuring the target for both sides. It was this phenomenon that gave rise to the expression 'fog of war', though it has come to mean much more since 1815. In battle, burning grains of powder caused 'powder burns' when they settled on the men's faces, arms and hands, while the smoke would blacken their skin with unburned powder residue. The fumes created by the multiple explosions also gave the men a raging thirst and could cause severe headaches – indeed, these were unavoidable in any event owing to the loud report of the guns, together with the shouts of the men and the rolling of the gun carriages. With ships at great risk from fire and explosion, the Yeoman of the Powder Room specifically monitored the gunpowder and ensured that it was stored and handled properly. To minimize the risk of fire, the powder charges were held in cylindrical wooden containers and taken up to the gun decks by 'powder monkeys' – nimble young boys who raced up and down the ladders as rapidly as possible.

Small arms

Members of a ship's crew could make use of a variety of hand-held weapons for close action, including firearms and edged weapons. The Board of Ordnance maintained an arsenal at the Tower of London, though civilian contractors also supplied the naval service with muskets and pistols. The former consisted of a shorter version of the land pattern musket, or 'Brown Bess', which measured 46in. in length, weighted 9lb 4oz., and fired a lead ball with a 0.75in. diameter. Muskets and pistols were not rifled, and thus suffered from the same deficiencies in accuracy as their smoothbore counterparts in naval ordnance. Effective range was at best 100 yards, though across a rolling deck all but a marksman was lucky to hit a man with an aimed shot. Writing in 1814, a colonel in the Army lamented that a musket ball:

> Will strike a figure of a man at 80 yards; it may even … at a 100, but a soldier must be very unfortunate indeed who shall be wounded by a common musket at 150 yards provided his antagonist aims at him: and as to firing at a man at 200 yards with a common musket you may as well fire at the moon and have the same hope of hitting your object. I do maintain and will prove whenever called upon that no man was ever killed at 200 yards by a common musket by the person who aimed at him.

Firearms were therefore used with best effect when ships stood practically side by side or during boarding, though once discharged they were rendered little better than clubs, for there was no time in the heat of a mêlée to reload them. This accounts for pistols always being issued in pairs. Shore duty, of course, was another matter, and for this task sailors were quite sensibly armed with muskets and bayonets.

British sailors (in blue) and marines (in red) boarding an enemy ship. Apart from the prestige attendant upon capturing an opposing vessel, sailors enjoyed the financial incentive of prize money, by which the Admiralty paid the victors a proportion of the value of the prize. (Stratford Archive)

Tactics

British naval strategy imparted numerous responsibilities upon the Royal Navy, including the seizing of the enemy's colonial resources, the defence of the nation from invasion and the protection of British supplies from overseas. Control of the sea was largely maintained by frigates, which could operate as reconnaissance vessels, perform convoy duty, and fight in ship-to-ship actions. Ships of the line did not cruise the seas in this manner, but rather performed blockade duty and, when possible, confronted the enemy in fleet actions. This, indeed, was a fleet's raison d'être: to bring a rival fleet to battle and destroy it.

Once engaged with the enemy, general strategy gave way to the more technical art of tactics – the actual methods employed to defeat the enemy in battle. British tactics were based on the line of battle, which required an admiral to draw up his fleet in one or two lines, usually with the flagship in the centre and the frigates stationed on the unopposed side, so distributed along the line as to be capable of repeating orders from the flagship to the rest of the fleet before the engagement began. The enemy would also form a line, and the British attack would come either obliquely or in parallel, with, theoretically, every ship engaging an opponent of equal or weaker strength. By employing such tactics, the maximum strength of each ship's broadside could be brought to bear. Prior to action, the admiral would already have decided whether he wished to attack with the weather gage or the lee gage. The side with the weather gage, by which the wind blew one's force in the direction of the enemy, could almost invariably make contact with an opponent, whether he wished to engage in combat or not. The side with the weather gage also provided the attacker with the opportunity to double the enemy's line (i.e. to attack him from both sides simultaneously) or pass through or break his line. On the other hand, the fleet with the lee gage could allow its weaker or damaged ships to leave the line when necessary. Moreover, the heel of the ship, which elevated the trajectory of the guns on the lower deck, allowed a vessel's lower-deck ports to remain open longer, and provided more opportunities for firing on the enemy, the angle of whose opposing guns being depressed would not allow continuous fire. In short, a fleet determined

Nelson explaining his battle plan to his captains prior to Trafalgar, October 1805. (Royal Naval Museum)

Enemy ships taken, burnt or sunk by the Royal Navy, 1793–1815	
(Approximate number of vessels mounting four or more guns)	
French losses, 1793–1802	370
French losses, 1803–15	310
Total	**680**
Dutch losses, 1795–1800	90
Dutch losses, 1803–10	40
Total	**130**
Spanish losses, 1796–1802	65
Spanish losses, 1804–08	60
Total	**125**
Danish losses, 1801	15
Danish losses, 1807–13	70
Total	**85**
Russian losses, 1808–09	4
Turkish losses, 1807–08	13
American losses, 1812–15	12

to engage an enemy always favoured the weather gage, whereas a fleet seeking the lee gage normally did so to be sure of surviving an action, not least through the option of escape.

In most of the major actions of the French Revolutionary and Napoleonic Wars the British sought to break or otherwise disrupt the enemy's line, and therefore sought the weather gage. Contrary to popular belief, the notion of breaking the enemy's line was not original to Nelson, nor even a product of the wars in which he fought; rather it originated with Admiral Rodney who, at the battle of the Saintes in 1782, penetrated the French line in an unprecedented feat later repeated in similar style at the Glorious First of June (1794), Camperdown (1797), St Vincent (1797) and, of course, most famously at Trafalgar (1805). In all these instances British tactics were invariably aggressive, with admirals and captains taking the initiative to attack, confident that their better-trained crews, even when faced by a numerically superior foe, would carry the day.

HMS *Java* (38) fights USS *Constitution* (44), on 29 December 1812, off Brazil. After a two-hour engagement, the wrecked *Java* struck her colours. (Stratford Archive)

1) Fleet in line of battle. This was the standard formation for attack, with each ship of the line (so-called because it was large enough to fight in the line of battle) drawn up bow to stern. The flagship, bearing the commander-in-chief, was positioned at approximately mid-point in the line to enable its signals to be seen clearly by the 'repeating' frigates. These were positioned to windward, so poised to be able to repeat the signals for the benefit of all the ships in the fleet.

2) The fleet to windward enjoyed the advantage of being able to choose the approximate time and point of attack. Here, the windward fleet approaches in an attempt to manoeuvre around the head of the enemy's line, so forcing it to accept battle.

3) The windward fleet attempts to engage an enemy which, positioned to leeward, has the option to avoid battle by turning away and fleeing with all its sails deployed.

4) The windward battlefleet successfully engages the enemy fleet, which is sailing to leeward.

5) Breaking the line. The attacking fleet passes through the opposing line in order to engage the enemy on both sides – a manoeuvre known as 'doubling'. This tactic was employed successfully by the British fleets at the Saintes (1782), St Vincent (1797) Camperdown (1797), the Nile (1798) and Trafalgar (1805).

6) Isolating the van. Having passed through the opposing line, the attacker isolates the enemy van, thus preventing him from escaping to leeward.

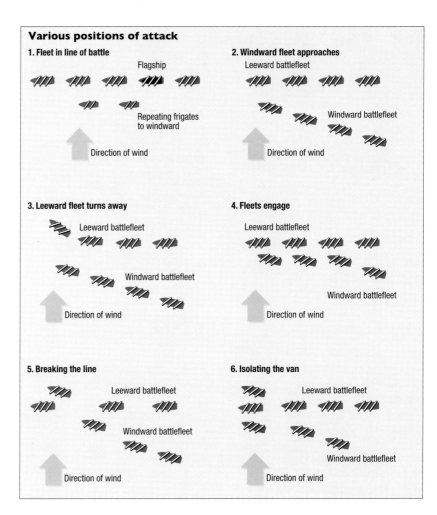

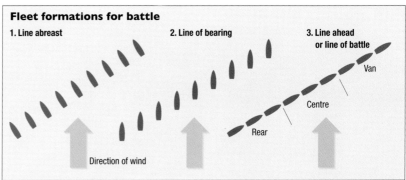

1) Line abreast was often adopted in waters where the presence of an enemy fleet was considered remote. Still, patrolling frigates positioned around the fleet performed the task of reconnoitring to ensure that an admiral was not caught unawares.

2) Line of bearing enabled ships both to communicate easily with each other and to form into line ahead with a minimum of time and effort.

3) Line ahead (also known as line of battle) had since the mid-17th century remained the standard method of deploying ships of the line preparing to engage the enemy. By the end of the 19th century, however, bolder, more innovative commanders such as Nelson had begun to depart from the Admiralty's official *Fighting Instructions* in order to break the enemy line and fight what he called a 'pell-mell' battle; that is, pitting individual ships against one another in scattered positions, relying on superior British gunnery and discipline to decide each contest and thus achieve a successful outcome for the battle as a whole.

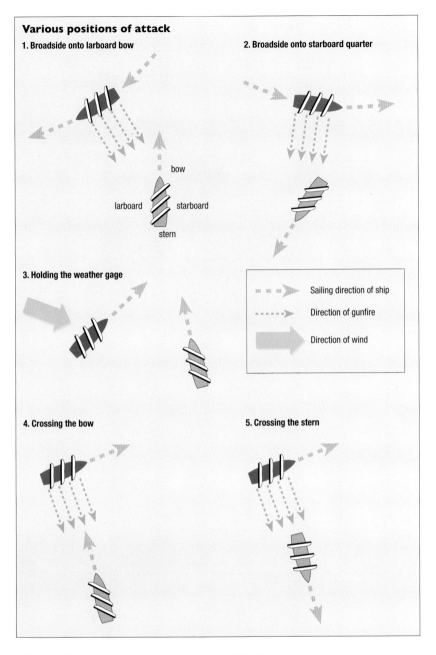

Various positions of attack

1. Broadside onto larboard bow

2. Broadside onto starboard quarter

bow

larboard   starboard

stern

3. Holding the weather gage

Sailing direction of ship

Direction of gunfire

Direction of wind

4. Crossing the bow

5. Crossing the stern

1–2) Broadside onto larboard bow and broadside onto starboard quarter. As shown here, vessels able to bring to bear their full broadside against an enemy whose position limited his own field of fire, enjoyed a significant tactical advantage. Thus, with skillful manoeuvring an attacker could maintain such a position – more often in a ship-to-ship, rather than in a fleet, action – so crippling an enemy whilst sustaining relatively little damage in return. It was precisely in such circumstances where superior seamanship, as opposed to superior gunnery, often told.

3) Holding the weather gage. A vessel so positioned enjoyed the advantage of determining the approximate time and place of engagement, though it could not usually prevent the enemy from avoiding battle if he so desired.

4–5) Crossing the bow and crossing the stern. These were the most effective positions of attack, especially the latter. Also known as crossing the 'T', this position enabled the attacker to fire with virtual impunity against the most vulnerable parts of the enemy vessel, above all the stern windows of the opposing captain's cabin. Round shot fired along the length of an enemy's lower decks inevitably caused frightful havoc, overturning guns and bowling over men like ninepins.

The Nile, 1–2 August 1798

The battle of the Nile was fought in Aboukir Bay on the Egyptian coast, approximately 15 miles east of the mouth of the Nile. Admiral Brueys, commanding the French Mediterranean Fleet, chose this open anchorage for his 13 ships of the line and four frigates, secure in the knowledge that his position was, if not unassailable, at least strong enough to prevent the British from dislodging him. Specifically, he deployed his ships in a close line near to a shoal, with his weaker van protected by a six-gun battery situated on a nearby island and his strongest vessels composing the centre and rear. His brigs and frigates, together with gunboats and bomb vessels, sat on the landward side where it was presumed they would enjoy protection from an attacker. This deployment seemed the most sensible option given the shape and depth of the harbour; indeed, it ought to have been had Brueys been opposed by a less

This shows the standard formation in battle, line ahead, the most effective means by which ships could bring their guns to bear against the enemy. Once engaged, however, such pristine formations could not necessarily be maintained, for damage, the enemy's movements, new signals from the commander, and the general chaos of battle could throw a battle line into disarray.

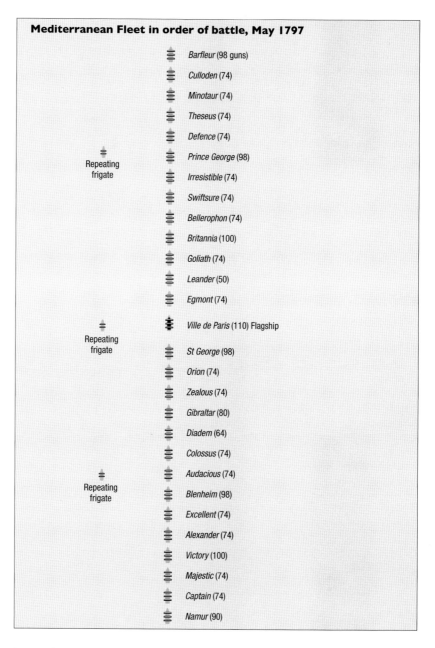

Mediterranean Fleet in order of battle, May 1797

Barfleur (98 guns)

Culloden (74)

Minotaur (74)

Theseus (74)

Defence (74)

Prince George (98)

Irresistible (74)

Swiftsure (74)

Bellerophon (74)

Britannia (100)

Goliath (74)

Leander (50)

Egmont (74)

Ville de Paris (110) Flagship

St George (98)

Orion (74)

Zealous (74)

Gibraltar (80)

Diadem (64)

Colossus (74)

Audacious (74)

Blenheim (98)

Excellent (74)

Alexander (74)

Victory (100)

Majestic (74)

Captain (74)

Namur (90)

Repeating frigate

Repeating frigate

Repeating frigate

intrepid opponent, for no sooner had Nelson entered the bay than he was advised by one of his captains of a fundamental flaw in the French defence.

Crucially, Brueys had been at anchor for a month and was not aware of Nelson's approach. As a result, hundreds of his men were ashore collecting water for the fleet. Nor did Brueys expect Nelson to attack so late in the day or believe his opponent's ships could negotiate the shoals that partially protected the opening of the harbour. In addition, dusk was already looming when the British fleet went into action – further cause for Brueys to assume Nelson would not attack until the following day. The French were also unprepared on their landward side, on the basis that their commander thought it impossible for the British to double his line owing to the shoals – the flaw identified by the British. Brueys did manage to clear for action on his starboard (i.e. seaward) side, but his captains had time before the British attacked around 1830hrs neither to put springs on their ships' cables – a procedure that would have enabled them to swing themselves into new positions – nor to bring up their stern anchors. The French were thus forced to fight in a static position and could do nothing to prevent the British from engaging from the landward side – a position thought to be too shallow for a ship of the line to negotiate.

Not only were the French crews under strength, but they had also stacked boxes, barrels and crates on the landward side of their decks, making it, at least initially, impossible to handle the guns on the port side. Appreciating that the enemy rear was in no position to assist the centre and van, Nelson concentrated his initial attack on only a portion of the French line, bringing for this purpose 13 ships (the fourteenth, HMS *Culloden*, had grounded on a shoal at the mouth of the harbour and took no part in the action) to engage only eight French. This numerical advantage, compounded by the superior rate of fire of the British crews, enabled Nelson to overwhelm each enemy ship in turn, and move successively down the line, disabling and capturing more vessels after fierce exchanges of fire. Not only could the ships composing the French rear offer no assistance to their consorts further up the line, but most of these eventually succumbed to the British onslaught, with only two ships of the line and two frigates managing to escape.

Trafalgar, 21 October 1805

At Trafalgar – unlike at the Nile, fought in the open sea – Nelson divided his fleet into two roughly equal-sized columns, one of which was to separate the Franco-Spanish centre and rear from their van. The other would pierce the enemy line through its centre. By doing so, the van would be unable to support its consorts without coming about – a process that could take so long that the battle might already be lost. By isolating the van, Nelson not only compensated for his own numerical inferiority (33 Franco-Spanish ships of the line to his 27), but also could then himself outnumber his opponents in the centre and rear. This form of attack entailed a certain degree of risk, however: the leading vessel of each column, by sailing directly against the enemy's broadsides, would receive fire against its stern without any means of reply until the line was reached. In the event, the *Victory* and the *Royal Sovereign* reached the enemy line without injuries serious enough to prevent them from passing through Admiral Villeneuve's line, against which a whole succession of British ships issued devastating broadsides while crossing the enemy's 'T'.

Once both columns broke through, Nelson relied on individual captains to engage the enemy's ships and capture or destroy them through superior gunnery, morale, discipline and seamanship. The admiral knew that once battle was joined, issuing new signals would probably be of little use, for they

The battle of Trafalgar, 21 October 1805. Nelson, with 27 ships of the line, smashed the combined Franco-Spanish fleet of 33 vessels in the most decisive naval encounter in modern history. (Umhey Collection)

The battle of the Nile, 1–2 August 1798, the most decisive naval encounter of the 18th century. In very few engagements, whether on land or sea, may one side genuinely be described as having been annihilated. At the Nile, British tactics proved so effective as to trap all but a handful of French vessels within the narrow confines of Aboukir Bay, with the opportunity for escape passing before the course of the battle turned – virtually from the outset – decisively in Nelson's favour.

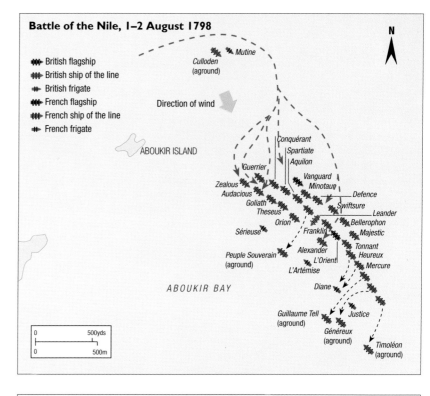

Battle of the Nile, 1–2 August 1798

- British flagship
- British ship of the line
- British frigate
- French flagship
- French ship of the line
- French frigate

Direction of wind

ABOUKIR ISLAND

N

Mutine
Culloden (aground)

Conquérant
Spartiate
Aquilon
Guerrier
Vanguard
Minotaur
Zealous
Audacious
Goliath
Theseus
Défence
Swiftsure
Leander
Orion
Bellerophon
Sérieuse
Franklin
Majestic
Peuple Souverain (aground)
Alexander
Tonnant
Heureux
L'Orient
Mercure
L'Artémise
Diane
Guillaume Tell (aground)
Justice
Généreux (aground)
Timoléon (aground)

ABOUKIR BAY

0   500yds
0   500m

Nelson chose to attack with two divisions of approximately equal strength, driving through the Franco-Spanish line in order to isolate and defeat the centre and rear before the van could make the wide turning movement required to enable it to assist its beleaguered consorts to the south. The British could rely with confidence on the notion that, once evenly matched in numerical terms because of the isolation of the enemy van, their ships would overwhelm their opponents in the inevitable slogging match that would develop once the Franco-Spanish line had been broken. Nevertheless, the line of approach adopted by the columns under Nelson and Collingwood, respectively, exposed their leading vessels to considerable danger, for whereas the defenders could concentrate their full broadsides against the bows of their attackers, the British could offer no reply until they reached the enemy line.

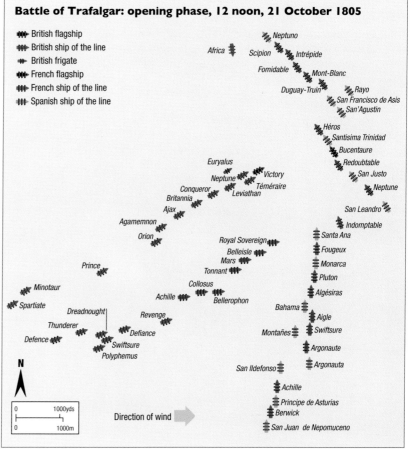

Battle of Trafalgar: opening phase, 12 noon, 21 October 1805

- British flagship
- British ship of the line
- British frigate
- French flagship
- French ship of the line
- Spanish ship of the line

Neptuno
Africa
Scipion
Intrépide
Fomidable
Mont-Blanc
Duguay-Truin
Rayo
San Francisco de Asis
San'Agustin
Héros
Santisima Trinidad
Bucentaure
Euryalus
Redoubtable
Neptune
Victory
San Justo
Conqueror
Téméraire
Neptune
Britannia
Leviathan
Ajax
San Leandro
Agamemnon
Indomptable
Orion
Santa Ana
Royal Sovereign
Fougeux
Belleisle
Monarca
Prince
Mars
Pluton
Tonnant
Algésiras
Minotaur
Collosus
Spartiate
Achille
Bellerophon
Bahama
Dreadnought
Revenge
Aigle
Thunderer
Montañes
Swiftsure
Defiance
Defence
Argonaute
Swiftsure
Argonauta
Polyphemus
San Ildefonso
Achille
Principe de Asturias
Berwick
Direction of wind
San Juan de Nepomuceno

N

0   1000yds
0   1000m

Men clinging to wreckage and fallen rigging during the battle of Trafalgar. Notwithstanding their intimate connection with the sea, very few sailors could actually swim. (Philip Haythornthwaite)

would probably be unseen in the smoke and confusion. It was for this reason that Nelson issued instructions which covered all contingencies: 'In case signals can neither be seen nor perfectly understood no captain can do very wrong if he places his ship alongside that of an enemy.' As expected, the fighting then developed into a series of ship-to-ship encounters – what the admiral called a 'pell-mell' battle – including several unsuccessful French attempts to board the *Victory* and other vessels. Very belatedly, the Franco-Spanish van attempted to wear and come to the assistance of the centre and rear, detaching ten vessels for the purpose. Ships from Collingwood's column, however, prevented Admiral Dumanoir Le Pelley from rescuing a hopeless situation by interposing themselves between the shattered centre and rear and the as yet unengaged Franco-Spanish van. The resulting British victory was nothing if not decisive: 18 enemy ships of the line captured or destroyed – more than half Villeneuve's force.

The brig HMS *Little Belt* and frigate USS *President* exchange fire, 16 May 1811, more than a year before hostilities broke out between the United States and Britain. Commodore John Rogers of the *President* had been sent to cruise off New York to prevent British ships from stopping and searching American vessels in pursuit of British seamen seeking to avoid service in the Royal Navy. Rodgers pursued and confronted the *Little Belt* but could not make contact until darkness had fallen. The British sloop refused to identify herself, whereupon a shot was fired – neither side laying claim to it – and a 30-minute action ensued, leaving 11 British dead and 21 wounded, to the Americans' single injured ship's boy. While Rodgers himself expressed regret for the action, his countrymen and government were growing increasingly irritated by the impressment of American citizens by Royal Navy captains. (Stratford Archive)

Genesis of battle: a first-hand account

The classic naval encounter between the 38-gun HMS *Macedonian* and the USS *United States* (44) in October 1812 as described by Samuel Leech gives a good impression of how a ship prepared for battle and actually fought.

A lookout high in the rigging, possibly perched on one of the tops (a platform fixed up each mast), indicated the presence of another vessel with the words, 'Sail ho!'. The captain immediately came on deck and called for the direction of the strange ship and enquired into its nationality. On hailing the lookout again, after a few minutes passed, he received the information he required. Once it was identified as an enemy – in this case an American – ship, the captain issued his command and the ship was readied for battle:

> All hands clear the ship for action, ahoy! The drum and fife beat to quarters; bulk-heads were knocked away; the guns were released from their confinement; the whole dread paraphernalia of battle was produced; and after a few minutes of hurry and confusion, every man and boy was at his post, ready to do his best service for his country ...

To ensure that every man remained at his respective station, the junior midshipmen were told to shoot anyone who deserted his post. The guns were loaded and the slow matches lit, in case the matchlocks misfired. A proportion of the men were then allocated the task of making up a boarding party, should one be required. Leech then described how:

> A lieutenant then passed through the ship, directing the marines and boarders, who were furnished with pikes, cutlasses, and pistols, [and told] how to proceed if it should be necessary to board the enemy. He was followed by the captain, who exhorted the men to fidelity and courage, urging upon their consideration the well-known motto of the brave Nelson, 'England expects [that] every man [will] do his duty'.

The men in the tops, usually responsible for working the sails, were issued with small arms so as to direct fire down on the enemy. Below, on the main deck, Leech was stationed at the fifth gun, where he was responsible for ensuring that his gun was supplied with powder by running up and down the ladders to and from the magazine with cartridges covered by his jacket. The ship was then manoeuvred to enable the starboard guns to come into action, with a telltale sound indicating the start of the engagement. Leech recorded that:

HMS *Guerriere* (38) v USS *Constitution* (44) one of several epic frigate actions fought during the Anglo-American War (1812–15). Contrary to popular belief, guns were not fired simultaneously as one thunderous broadside, except perhaps for the opening salvo, for the shock to the ship and crew would be extremely great. Guns were normally fired on the orders of individual gun captains who timed ignition according to the moment during the constant roll of the ship when their guns came to bear on the enemy. (Stratford Archive)

A strange noise, such as I had never heard before, next arrested my attention; it sounded like the tearing of sails, just over our heads. This I soon ascertained to be the wind of the enemy's shot. The firing, after a few minutes' cessation, recommenced. The roaring of cannon could now be heard from all parts of our trembling ship, and, mingling as it did with that of our foes, it made a most hideous noise. By-and-by I heard the shot strike the sides of our ship; the whole scene grew indescribably confused and horrible; it was like some awfully tremendous thunder-storm, whose deafening roar is attended by incessant streaks of lightning, carrying death in every flash and strewing the ground with the victims of its wrath; only, in our case, the scene was rendered more horrible than that, by the presence of torrents of blood which dyed our decks.

Throughout the fight Leech heard the cries of the wounded all around him – some men dismembered by shot and others disfigured by flying splinters. The wounded were carried below to the cockpit, the dead heaved overboard. One of the powder monkeys was severely burned in the face when a cartridge in his hands caught fire. 'In this pitiable situation,' Leech wrote, 'the agonized boy lifted up both hands, as if imploring relief, when a passing shot instantly cut him in two.' One of the other members of the gun crew lost his hands to a passing shot, followed by a second which opened his bowels. With no hope of survival, he was thrown overboard by his comrades:

Such was the terrible scene, amid which we kept on our shouting and firing. Our men fought like tigers. Some of them pulled off their jackets, others their jackets and vests; while some, still more determined, had taken off their shirts, and, with nothing but a handkerchief tied round the waistbands of their trowsers, fought like heroes.

Men aboard ship, frightened though they might have been, had no means of escape from the combination of shouts, screams, smoke and the roar of gunfire. There was little choice but to carry out the tasks for which they had been trained, as Leech further observed:

We all appeared cheerful, but I know that many a serious thought ran through my mind … To run from our quarters would have been certain death from the hands of our own officers; to give way to gloom, or to show fear, would do no good, and might brand us with the name of cowards, and ensure certain defeat. Our only true philosophy, therefore, was to make the best of our situation by fighting bravely and cheerfully.

Soldiers and sailors throughout history have sought protection in battle through prayer. Even those, like Leech, who had no particular religious dispositions, still sought divine intervention when faced with the imminent prospect of death:

I thought a great deal … of the other world; every groan, every falling man, told me that the next instant I might be before the Judge of all the earth. For this, I felt unprepared; but being without any particular knowledge of religious truth, I satisfied myself by repeating again and again the Lord's prayer and promising that if spared I would be more attentive to religious duties than ever before. This promise I had no doubt, at the time, of keeping; but I have learned since that it is easier to make promises amidst the roar of the battle's thunder, or in the horrors of shipwreck, than to keep them when danger is absent and safety smiles upon our path.

As fate would have it, her American adversary easily outgunned the *Macedonian*, and Leech, together with the remainder of the crew, was taken prisoner.

Conclusion

In the course of the French Revolutionary and Napoleonic Wars the Royal Navy reached the climax of its effectiveness as a fighting force. So comprehensive was its record of success that by the conclusion of these conflicts every French colony had fallen into British hands and every French port was under effective blockade. The standards of gunnery, discipline and seamanship attained as a result of regular training, and the constant vigilance and the attentiveness of its officers, enabled the Royal Navy to outfight any opponent, and when Britain emerged in 1815 as the dominant power on the seas it was a position she would hold unchallenged for the next century.

But the Navy's success may be attributed to more than the men and ships themselves; for the level of resources that the nation committed for its maintenance played an important role in the Navy's record of achievement. Although its manpower needs were never satisfied, the Navy easily absorbed the largest proportion of the national budget. Both Parliament and the government appreciated that the nation's prosperity and, indeed, its very existence, depended on the maintenance of a navy superior to all others, and thus they were prepared generously to fund it – even if those funds fell short of what every Lord of the Admiralty and serving officer and rating would have liked. In protecting Britain's trade across the world, the Navy ensured that the country could generate the funds needed to maintain a maritime force of unprecedented size. Britain's sound financial base, in turn, enabled the government to borrow heavily to support the Navy, an institution with no rival in terms of technical complexity, administrative support, and cost.

It is remarkable that in a conflict lasting over 20 years little in the way of technological innovation should have occurred. Nor indeed was the age noted for a substantial transformation of tactics. It was, however, a time when Britain produced a multitude of fine commanders at all levels, only the most senior of whom are properly commemorated – men like Nelson, Collingwood, Smith, Saumarez, Duncan, St Vincent, Howe, Cochrane and others. Dozens of lesser-known and in most cases, unrecognized, officers displayed extraordinary skill and devotion to service. Under them, tens of thousands of seamen and marines spent years on blockade duty, protecting trade, fighting privateers and seeking to bring (and, on occasion, actually bringing) the enemy's fleet to battle – in so doing producing the most powerful navy hitherto known.

British ships in action at Trafalgar. In seeking to separate the Franco-Spanish centre and rear from its van, Nelson issued the following instructions prior to battle: 'If the enemy's fleet should be seen to windward in line of battle ... they will probably be so extended that their van could not succour their rear. I should therefore probably make the second in command's signal to lead through, about their 12th ship from the rear ... My line would cut through about their centre ... The whole impression of the British fleet must be to overpower [from] two or three ships ahead of their commander-in-chief, supposed to be in the centre, to the rear of the fleet. I will suppose 20 sail of the enemy's line to be untouched; it must be some time before they could perform a manoeuvre to bring their force compact to attack any part of the British fleet engaged, or to succour their own ships.' (Stratford Archive)

Orders of battle

The Glorious First of June, 1 June 1794

The first fleet action of the French Revolutionary Wars was actually fought over five days, but culminated in a major encounter on 1 June 1794. Fought 400 miles off Ushant, west of the Breton Peninsula, between Admiral Earl Howe with 34 ships of the line and Rear-Admiral Villaret-Joyeuse with 30 ships, Howe's objective was to intercept an immense grain convoy from America bound for the starving population of France. In the event, Howe attacked and took six enemy ships, while a seventh foundered. More could have been achieved had the British pursued, but their crews were exhausted and Howe remained content to claim only a tactical victory, failing as he had to prevent the vital convoy reaching Brest.

Caesar	80	Captain Anthony Molloy
Bellerophon	74	Rear-Admiral Thomas Pasley
		Captain William Hope
Leviathan	74	Captain Lord Hugh Seymour
Russell	74	Captain John Payne
Royal Sovereign	100	Vice-Admiral Thomas Graves
		Captain Henry Nicholls
Marlborough	74	Captain Hon. George Berkeley
Defence	74	Captain James Gambier
Impregnable	98	Rear-Admiral Benjamin Caldwell
		Captain George Westcott
Tremendous	74	Captain James Pigott
Barfleur	98	Rear-Admiral George Bowyer
		Captain Cuthbert Collingwood
Invincible	74	Captain Hon Thomas Pakenham
Culloden	74	Captain Isaac Schomberg
Gibraltar	80	Captain Thomas Mackenzie
Queen Charlotte	100	Admiral Earl Howe
		Captain Sir Roger Curtis
		Captain Sir Andrew Douglas
Brunswick	74	Captain John Harvey
Valiant	74	Captain Thomas Pringle
Orion	74	Captain John Duckworth
Queen	98	Rear-Admiral Alan Gardner
		Captain John Hutt
Ramillies	74	Captain Henry Harvey
Alfred	74	Captain John Bazely
Montagu	74	Captain James Montagu
Royal George	100	Vice-Admiral Sir Alexander Hood
		Captain William Domett
Majestic	74	Captain Charles Cotton
Glory	98	Captain John Elphinstone
Thunderer	74	Captain Albermarle Bertie
Phaeton	38	Captain William Bentinck
Latona	38	Captain Edward Thornbrough
Niger	32	Captain Hon. Arthur Legge
Southampton	32	Captain Hon. Robert Forbes

Venus	32	Captain William Brown
Aquilon	32	Captain Hon. Robert Stopford
Pegasus	32	Captain Robert Barlow

The Gulf of Genoa, 13–14 March 1795

Vice-Admiral William Hotham, commander of the British fleet in the Mediterranean, followed 15 French ships of the line under Rear-Admiral Martin, steering for Corsica with 5,000 troops to retake the island. After two days of ineffective manoeuvring, Hotham finally closed when two French ships became fouled, fell astern and suffered severe damage from British fire. The following morning the two fleets engaged at long range but with no decisive result, the French escaping to the west by mid-afternoon, abandoning the crippled *Ça Ira* and *Censeur*, which had taken the former in tow, to capture.

Van:
Captain	74	Captain Samuel Reeve
Bedford	74	Captain Davidge Gould
Tancredi (Neap.)	74	Captain Chev. Caraccioli
Princess Royal	98	Vice-Admiral Samuel Goodall
		Captain John Purvis
Agamemnon	64	Captain Horatio Nelson
Minerva (Neap.)	32	--
Pilade (Neap.)	--	--
Lowestoft	32	Captain Benjamin Hallowell
Poulette	26	Commander Ralph Miller
Tarleton	14	Captain Charles Brisbane

Centre:
Illustrious	74	Captain Thomas Frederick
Courageux	74	Captain Augustus Montgomery
Britannia	100	Vice-Admiral William Hotham
		Captain John Holloway
Egmont	74	Captain John Sutton
Windsor Castle	98	Rear-Admiral Robert Linzee
		Captain John Gore
Inconstant	36	Captain Thomas Fremantle
Meleager	32	Captain George Cockburn

Rear:
Diadem	64	Captain Charles Tyler
St George	98	Vice-Admiral Sir Hyde Parker
		Captain Thomas Foley
Terrible	74	Captain George Campell
Fortitude	74	Captain William Young
Romulus	36	Captain George Hope
Moselle	18	Commander Charles Pater
Fox	cutter	Lieutenant John Gibson

Belle Isle, 17 June 1795

A running engagement fought north of Belle Isle in the Bay of Biscay, where a formidable French squadron of 12 ships of the line, two 50-gun ships and nine frigates under Admiral Villaret-Joyeuse pursued a retreating British force of five ships of the line and two frigates under Vice-Admiral William Cornwallis. The *Mars*, having fallen astern as a result of damaged rigging, narrowly avoided capture when Cornwallis interposed the *Royal Sovereign* and saved her. Meanwhile, believing that the main British fleet was at hand after the frigate *Phaeton* issued false signals as a ruse, the French broke off the action.

Royal Sovereign	100	Vice-Admiral Hon. William Cornwallis
		Captain John Whitby
Mars	74	Captain Sir Charles Cotton
Triumph	74	Captain Sir Erasmus Gower
Brunswick	74	Captain Lord Charles Fitzgerald
Bellerophon	74	Captain James, Lord Cranstoun
Phaeton	38	Captain Hon. Robert Stopford
Pallas	32	Captain Hon. Henry Curzon
Kingfisher	18	Commander Thomas Gosselin

Ile de Groix, 23 June 1795

Lord Bridport, commander of the Channel Fleet with 14 ships of the line, sighted a French squadron of nine ships of the line under Admiral Villaret-Joyeuse, which immediately retreated towards Lorient. A general engagement began when the British van overtook the French off Ile de Groix off the Breton coast. The French failed to maintain a cohesive formation and three of their ships surrendered. Bridport, content merely to claim these prizes, broke off action, enabling Villaret-Joyeuse to reach Lorient with his remaining force.

Royal George	100	Admiral Lord Bridport
		Captain William Domett
Queen Charlotte	100	Captain Sir Andrew Douglas
Queen	98	Vice-Admiral Alan Gardner
		Captain William Bedford
London	98	Vice-Admiral John Colpoys
		Captain Edward Griffith
Prince of Wales	98	Rear-Admiral Henry Harvey
		Captain John Bazely
Prince	98	Captain Charles Hamilton
Barfleur	98	Captain James Dacres
Prince George	98	Captain William Edge
Sans Pareil	80	Rear-Admiral Lord Hugh Seymour
		Captain William Browell
Valiant	74	Captain Christopher Parker
Orion	74	Captain Sir James Saumarez
Irresistible	74	Captain Richard Grindall
Russell	74	Captain Thomas Larcom
Colossus	74	Captain John Monkton
Révolutionnaire	44	Captain Francis Cole
Thalia	36	Captain Lord Henry Paulet
Nymphe	36	Captain George Murray
Aquilon	32	Robert Barlow
Astroea	32	Captain Richard Lane
Babet	20	Captain Edward Codrington
Megoera	14	Hon. Henry Blackwood
Incendiary	14	Captain John Draper
Charon	44	Commander Walter Locke (hospital ship)
Argus	14	--
Dolly	14	--

Hyères, 13 July 1795

The second encounter between Vice-Admiral Hotham, commander of the British fleet in the Mediterranean, and his French counterpart, in 1795. Although Hotham enjoyed a numerical superiority of 23 ships of the line to Martin's 17, the British admiral acted indecisively when the two fleets met off the coast of Provence. Martin sought to avoid an encounter, while Hotham pursued. Both fleets were widely dispersed, and only the British van engaged their opponents, taking a 74 in the process. Fearing that the changing wind would blow him ashore, Hotham broke off the action.

Britannia	100	Admiral William Hotham
		Captain John Holloway
Victory	100	Rear-Admiral Robert Man
		Captain John Knight
Princess Royal	98	Vice-Admiral Samuel Goodall
		Captain John Purvis
St George	98	Vice-Admiral Sir Hyde Parker
		Captain Thomas Foley
Windsor Castle	98	Vice-Admiral Robert Linzee
		Captain John Gore
Blenheim	90	Captain John Bazely
Gibraltar	80	Captain John Pakenham
Captain	74	Captain Samuel Reeve
Fortitude	74	Captain William Young
Bombay Castle	74	Captain Charles Chamberlayne
Saturn	74	Captain James Douglas
Cumberland	74	Captain Bartholomew Rowley
Terrible	74	Captain George Campbell
Defence	74	Captain Thomas Wells
Egmont	74	Captain John Sutton
Culloden	74	Captain Thomas Troubridge
Bedford	74	Captain David Gould
Courageux	74	Captain Benjamin Hallowell
Audacious	74	Captain William Shield
Guiscardo (Neap)	74	--
Samnita (Neap)	74	--
Agamemnon	64	Commodore Horatio Nelson
Diadem	64	Captain Charles Tyler
Meleager	32	Captain George Cockburn
Cyclops	28	Captain William Hotham
Ariadne	24	Captain Robert Plampin
Comet	14	--
Éclair	20	--
Flèche	20	Commander Thomas Boys
Resolution	cutter	--
Moselle	18	Commander Charles Brisbane
Mutine	12	--

St Vincent, 14 February 1797

Admiral Jervis, leading the Mediterranean Fleet, decisively defeated a Spanish force twice his size, foiling Spanish efforts to link up with the French in Brest in preparation for a projected expedition against Ireland. The Spanish under Admiral de Cordova were arrayed in two divisions between which Jervis boldly sailed his fleet in a single column before turning to attack the Spanish weather division. Cordova, caught unawares, fought in a confused fashion before attempting to escape northwards. Commodore Horatio Nelson, commanding the third ship from the British rear and seeking to confound the Spanish escape, suddenly left the line and brought his ship straight into the path of the Spanish, taking on several large vessels in the process. The Spanish were obliged to alter course, and in the ensuing fight Jervis was able to bring up his remaining force. Cordova lost four vessels captured, two of these by Nelson and his crew.

Culloden	74	Captain Thomas Troubridge
Blenheim	98	Captain Thomas Frederick

Prince George	98	Rear-Admiral William Parker
		Captain John Irwin
Orion	74	Captain Sir James Saumarez
Colossus	74	Captain George Murray
Irresistible	74	Captain George Martin
Victory	100	Admiral Sir John Jervis
		Captain (1st) Robert Calder
		Captain (2nd) George Grey
Egmont	74	Captain John Sutton
Goliath	74	Captain Sir Charles Knowles
Barfleur	98	Vice-Admiral Hon. William Waldegrave
		Captain James Dacres
Britannia	100	Vice-Admiral Charles Thompson
		Captain Thomas Foley
Namur	90	Captain James Whitshed
Captain	74	Commodore Horatio Nelson
		Captain Ralph Miller
Diadem	64	Captain George Towry
Excellent	74	Captain Cuthbert Collingwood
Minerve	38	Captain George Cockburn
Southampton	32	Captain James Macnamara
Lively	32	Captain Lord Garlies
Niger	32	Captain Edward Foote
Bonne Citoyenne	20	Commander Charles Lindsay
Raven	18	Captain William Prowse
Fox	10	Lieutenant John Gibson

Camperdown, 11 October 1797

In early October 1797 the Dutch fleet of 16 ships of the line under Admiral de Winter emerged from Texel, upon which Admiral Duncan, with an equal force, left Yarmouth road to engage this force. Duncan deployed his fleet in two columns in line ahead, the weather division cutting through the rear of the Dutch line and capturing, after a two-hour fight, four ships exceeding 50 guns each and a frigate. At the same time, the lee division, under Duncan, attacked the Dutch van in a vicious three-and-a-half hour engagement, which ended with the capture of four more Dutch ships. Damage and casualties were severe on both sides.

Russell	74	Captain Henry Trollope
Director	64	Captain William Bligh
Montagu	74	Captain John Knight
Veteran	64	Captain George Gregory
Monarch	74	Vice-Admiral Richard Onslow
		Captain Edward O'Brien
Powerful	74	Captain William Drury
Monmouth	64	Commander James Walker, acting
Agincourt	64	Captain John Williamson
Triumph	74	Captain William Essington
Venerable	74	Admiral Adam Duncan
		Captain William Fairfax
Ardent	64	Captain Richard Burges
Bedford	74	Captain Sir Thomas Byard
Lancaster	64	Captain John Wells
Belliqueux	64	Captain John Inglis
Adamant	50	Captain William Hotham
Isis	50	Captain William Mitchell
Beaulieu	40	Captain Francis Fayerman
Circe	28	Captain Peter Halkett

Martin	16	Commander Hon Charles Paget
Rose	10	Lieutenant Joseph Brodie
King George	12	Lieutenant James Rains
Active	12	Lieutenant J. Hamilton
Diligent	12	Lieutenant T. Dawson
Speculator	8	Lieutenant H. Hales

The Nile, 1–2 August 1798

Having searched the Mediterranean for Admiral Brueys's fleet for three months, Rear-Admiral Sir Horatio Nelson finally discovered it anchored in line ahead in Aboukir Bay, 15 miles east of Alexandria on the Egyptian coast. With the advantage of surprise, Nelson sailed his 13 ships of the line into the bay to engage the enemy's 14 both from the landward and seaward sides. Concentrating their fire on the van and centre, the British systematically destroyed the French fleet, the flagship blowing up shortly after 2200hrs. The French lost 11 ships of the line and two frigates captured or destroyed, with only two ships of the line and two frigates managing to escape.

Goliath	74	Captain Thomas Foley
Zealous	74	Captain Samuel Hood
Orion	74	Captain Sir James Saumarez
Audacious	74	Captain Davidge Gould
Theseus	74	Captain Ralph Miller
Vanguard	74	Rear-Admiral Sir Horatio Nelson
		Captain Edward Berry
Minotaur	74	Captain Thomas Louis
Defence	74	Captain John Peyton
Bellerophon	74	Captain Henry Darby
Majestic	74	Captain George Westcott
Leander	50	Captain Thomas Thompson
Alexander	74	Captain Alexander Ball
Swiftsure	74	Captain Benjamin Hallowell
Culloden	74	Captain Thomas Troubridge
Mutine	16	Commander Thomas Hardy

Donegal, 12 October 1798

In an attempt to land troops in Ireland in 1798, the French under Commodore Bompart left Brest with one ship of the line, nine frigates and 3,000 troops. A squadron under Commodore Sir John Warren consisting of three ships of the line and five frigates discovered the French off Donegal and captured the *Hoche* (74) and three 36s. Pursuit of the remaining ships yielded three more frigates a few days later. The three remaining vessels reached France, but the loss of Bompart's squadron spelled the end of French support for the Irish revolutionaries.

Canada	74	Commodore Sir John Warren
Foudroyant	80	Captain Sir Thomas Byard
Robust	74	Captain Edward Thornbrough
Magnanime	44	Captain Hon. Michael de Courcy
Anson	44	Captain Philip Durham
Amelia	44	Captain Hon. Charles Herbert
Ethalion	38	Captain George Countess
Melampus	36	Captain Graham Moore

Copenhagen, 2 April 1801

In an effort to force the Danes from the League of Armed Neutrality, a British fleet under Admiral Sir Hyde Parker confronted the anchored Danish fleet of

18 ships of the line, plus hulks and floating batteries, the whole supported by formidable harbour defences. Parker's second in command, Vice-Admiral Nelson, with 10 ships of the line, two vessels of 50 and 54 guns respectively, plus a variety of frigates, sloops, bomb vessels and fireships, exchanged a ferocious fire in a four-hour slogging match in which both sides suffered severe damage and heavy casualties. The Danish fleet was neutralized and the League collapsed.

Elephant	74	Vice-Admiral Lord Nelson
		Captain Thomas Foley
Defiance	74	Rear-Admiral Thomas Graves
		Captain Richard Retalick
Edgar	74	Captain George Murray
Monarch	74	Captain James Mosse
Bellona	74	Captain Sir Thomas Thompson
Ganges	74	Captain Thomas Fremantle
Russell	74	Captain William Cuming
Agamemnon	64	Captain Robert Fancourt
Ardent	64	Captain Thomas Bertie
Polyphemus	64	Captain John Lawford
Glatton	54	Captain William Bligh
Isis	50	Captain James Walker
Amazon	38	Captain Edward Riou
Désirée	40	Captain Henry Inman
Blanche	36	Captain Graham Hamond
Alcmène	32	Captain Samuel Sutton
Jamaica	26	Captain Jonas Rose
Arrow	30	Captain William Bolton
Dart	30	Captain John Devonshire
Cruiser	18	Commander James Brisbane
Harpy	18	Commander William Birchall
Discovery	16	Commander John Conn (bomb vessel)
Explosion	8	Commander John Martin (bomb vessel)
Hecla	10	Commander Richard Hatherill
		(bomb vessel)
Sulphur	10	Commander Hender Whitter
		(bomb vessel)
Terror	8	Commander Samuel Rowley
		(bomb vessel)
Volcano	8	Commander James Watson
		(bomb vessel)
Zebra	16	Commander Edward Clay (bomb vessel)
Otter	14	Commander George M'Kinley (fireship)
Zephyr	14	Commander Clotworthy Upton (fireship)

First Algeciras, 6 July 1801

Fought off Gibraltar between Rear-Admiral Sir James Saumarez and a Franco-Spanish squadron under Admiral Linois. The British had six ships of the line to oppose three ships of the line and one frigate at their anchorage in Algeciras Bay. Linois was obliged to run his ships ashore, though Saumarez lost the *Hannibal* (74) when she ran aground near Spanish fortifications and was obliged to surrender. Putting into Gibraltar to effect very rapid repairs to his heavily damaged ships, Saumarez again put to sea in order to engage Linois a second time.

Caesar	80	Rear-Admiral Sir James Saumarez
		Captain Jahleel Brenton

Pompée	74	Captain Charles Stirling
Spencer	74	Captain Henry Darby
Venerable	74	Captain Samuel Hood
Hannibal	74	Captain Solomon Ferris
Audacious	74	Captain Shuldham Peard

Second Algeciras, 12–13 July 1801

In his second action in a week, Saumarez, with six ships of the line, took on a Franco-Spanish squadron of eight ships of the line and three frigates under admirals Linois and Moreno. The fighting began after dark on 12 July and carried on through the night. Two Spanish ships of the line caught fire and collided around midnight before sinking with immense losses. Shortly thereafter a French 74 was captured. Notwithstanding serious damage to several of his ships, Saumarez managed to reach Gibraltar safely with his prizes.

Caesar	80	Rear-Admiral Sir James Suamarez
		Captain Jahleel Brenton
Venerable	74	Captain Samuel Hood
Superb	74	Captain Richard Keats
Spencer	74	Captain Henry Darby
Audacious	74	Captain Shuldham Peard
Thames	32	Captain Aiskew Hollis
Carlotta (Portuguese)	--	Captain Craufurd Duncan
Calpe	14	Commander Hon. George Dundas
Louis	armed brig	Lieutenant Francis Truscott

Finisterre, 22 July 1805 (Calder's Action)

In a prelude to Trafalgar, Vice-Admiral Sir Robert Calder, stationed off Ferrol on the northern Spanish coast with 15 ships of the line, was ordered to intercept the squadron under Admiral Villeneuve, which had returned to European waters from the West Indies, in order to prevent its junction with the Spanish squadron in Ferrol. Heavy fog delayed fighting until evening, when an indecisive encounter followed in which the British temporarily prevented the French from reaching port. Calder took two Spanish ships of the line, but was later roundly criticized for failing to achieve greater success.

Hero	74	Captain Hon. Alan Gardner
Ajax	74	Captain William Brown
Triumph	74	Captain Henry Inman
Barfleur	98	Captain George Martin
Agamemnon	64	Captain John Harvey
Windsor Castle	98	Captain Charles Boyles
Defiance	74	Captain Philip Durham
Prince of Wales	98	Vice-Admiral Sir Robert Calder
		Captain William Cuming
Repulse	74	Captain Hon. Arthur Legge
Raisonnable	64	Captain Josias Rowley
Dragon	74	Captain Edward Griffith
Glory	98	Rear-Admiral Charles Stirling
		Captain Samuel Warren
Warrior	74	Captain Samuel Linzee
Thunderer	74	Captain William Lechmere
Malta	80	Captain Edward Buller
Egyptienne	40	Captain Hon. Charles Fleeming
Sirius	36	Captain William Prowse
Nile	lugger	Lieutenant John Fennell
Frisk	cutter	Lieutenant James Nicolson

Trafalgar, 21 October 1805

The most decisive naval battle of modern times, fought between a British fleet of 27 ships of the line under Vice-Admiral Lord Nelson, and a combined Franco-Spanish fleet of 33 ships (18 French, and 15 Spanish under Admiral Gravina) under Admiral Villeneuve. When the Combined Fleet left Cadiz, bound for the Mediterranean, Nelson pursued, dividing his fleet into two columns – the van or weather division – under himself, and the lee division under Vice-Admiral Collingwood. In an action lasting five hours the two British columns pierced the Franco-Spanish line and forced upon their opponents a series of spirited ship-to-ship actions in which superior British gunnery and seamanship wrecked Villeneuve's centre and rear before his van could come about and retrieve the situation. All told, the Combined Fleet lost 18 ships of the line captured or destroyed and over 6,000 men killed and wounded.

Victory	100	Vice-Admiral Lord Nelson
		Captain Thomas Hardy
Téméraire	98	Captain Eliab Harvey
Neptune	98	Captain Thomas Fremantle
Leviathan	74	Captain Henry Bayntun
Britannia	100	Rear-Admiral William, Earl of Northesk
		Captain Charles Bullen
Conqueror	74	Captain Israel Pellew
Africa	64	Captain Henry Digby
Agamemnon	64	Captain Sir Edward Berry
Ajax	74	Lieutenant John Pilfold (acting for Captain William Brown)
Orion	74	Captain Edward Codrington
Minotaur	74	Captain Charles Mansfield
Spartiate	74	Captain Sir Francis Laforey
Royal Sovereign	100	Vice-Admiral Cuthbert Collingwood
		Captain Edward Rotheram
Belleisle	74	Captain William Hargood
Mars	74	Captain George Duff
Tonnant	80	Captain Charles Tyler
Bellerophon	74	Captain John Cooke
Colossus	74	Captain James Morris
Achille	74	Captain Richard King
Dreadnought	98	Captain John Conn
Polyphemus	64	Captain Robert Redmill
Revenge	74	Captain Robert Moorsom
Swiftsure	74	Captain William Rutherfurd
Defiance	74	Captain Philip Durham
Thunderer	74	Lieutenant John Stockham (acting for Captain William Lechmere)
Defence	74	Captain George Hope
Prince	98	Captain Richard Grindall
Euryalus	36	Captain Hon. Henry Blackwood
Naiad	38	Captain Thomas Dundas
Phoebe	36	Captain Hon. Thomas Capell
Sirius	36	Captain William Prowse
Pickle	10	Lieutenant John La Penotière
Entreprenante	8	Lieutenant Robert Young

Cape Ortegal, 4 November 1805 (Strachan's Action)

Fought off the north-west coast of Spain two weeks after Trafalgar, when

Captain Sir Richard Strachan, with four ships of the line and four frigates, chased and engaged four ships of the line which had escaped from Trafalgar. When the British frigates caught up with the slowest enemy vessel, Rear-Admiral Dumanoir Le Pelley came about to do battle. Every French ship was dismasted in the ensuing mêlée, and after suffering appalling losses struck their colours.

Caesar	80	Captain Sir Richard Strachan
Hero	74	Captain Hon. Alan Gardner
Courageux	74	Captain Richard Lee
Namur	74	Captain Lawrence Halsted
Santa Margarita	36	Captain Wilson Rathborne
Aeolus	32	Captain Lord William Fitzroy
Phoenix	36	Captain Thomas Baker
Révolutionnaire	38	Captain Hon. Henry Hotham

San Domingo, 6 February 1806

Fought off Hispaniola in the West Indies three months after Trafalgar. Having eluded the blockade of Brest and escaped into the Atlantic, Rear-Admiral Leissègues with a French squadron found himself pursued all the way to the West Indies by a British force under Vice-Admiral Sir John Duckworth. Joined by reinforcements at Barbados, Duckworth with six ships of the line and two frigates made for Hispaniola where he discovered the French off the eastern coast of the island. In an action lasting only an hour and a half, two French ships of the line were driven ashore and later burnt, while Duckworth captured the other two. Only the two French frigates escaped.

Superb	74	Vice-Admiral Sir John Thomas Duckworth
		Captain Richard Keats
Canopus	80	Rear-Admiral Thomas Louis
		Captain Francis William Austen
Spencer	74	Captain Hon. Robert Stopford
Donegal	74	Captain Pulteney Malcolm
Northumberland	74	Rear-Admiral Hon. Alexander Cochrane
		Captain John Morrison
Atlas	74	Captain Samuel Pym
Agamemnon	64	Captain Sir Edward Berry
Acasta	40	Captain Richard Dunn
Magicienne	36	Captain Adam Mackenzie
Kingfisher	16	Commander Nathaniel Cochrane
Epervier	14	Lieutenant James Higginson

Basque and Aix Roads, 11–16 April 1809

Following Rear-Admiral Willaumez into the anchorage of Basque and Aix Roads near Rochefort, Admiral Gambier proceeded to blockade his adversary. Shortly thereafter Lord Cochrane arrived with a strong force of fireships and explosion vessels, each packed with hundreds of barrels of gunpowder. With wind and tide in his favour, Cochrane led the attack, forcing many French ships to cut their cables. Some vessels fouled each other and ran aground, but Gambier refused timely assistance to Cochrane and only four French ships of the line were captured or burnt. Further British attacks over the ensuing days were less successful once the element of surprise was lost.

Caledonia	120	Admiral Lord Gambier
		Captain Sir Harry Neale (1st captain)
		Captain William Bedford (2nd captain)

Caesar	80	Rear-Admiral Hon. Robert Stopford
		Captain Charles Richardson
Gibraltar	80	Captain Henry Ball
Hero	74	Captain James Newman
Donegal	74	Captain Pulteney Malcolm
Resolution	74	Captain George Burlton
Theseus	74	Captain John Beresford
Valiant	74	Captain John Bligh
Illustrious	74	Captain William Broughton
Bellona	74	Captain Stair Douglas
Revenge	74	Captain Alexander Kerr
Indefatigable	44	Captain John Rodd
Imperieuse	38	Captain Lord Cochrane
Amelia	38	Captain Hon. Frederick Irby
Aigle	36	Captain George Wolfe
Emerald	36	Captain Frederick Maitland
Unicorn	32	Captain Lucius Hardyman
Pallas	32	Captain George Seymour
Mediator	32	Commander James Wooldridge
Beagle	18	Commander Francis Newcombe
Doterel	18	Commander Anthony Abdy
Foxhound	18	Commander Pitt Greene
Lyra	10	Commander William Bevians
Redpole	10	Captain John Joyce
Thunderer	8	Commander James Caulfield (bomb vessel)
Aetna	8	Commander William Godfrey (bomb vessel)
Insolent	14	Lieutenant John Morris
Encounter	14	Lieutenant James Talbot
Conflict	12	Lieutenant Joseph Batt
Contest	14	Lieutenant John Gregory
Fervent	12	Lieutenant John Hare
Growler	14	Lieutenant Richard Crossman
Martial	14	Lieutenant Joseph Marrett
Whiting	4	Lieutenant Henry Wildey
Nimrod	hired cutter	Master's Mate Edward Tapley
King George	hired cutter	Master's Mate Thomas Mercer

Plus *Cleveland* (20) (transport vessel), 20 fireships, three explosion vessels, storeships and other vessels

Lissa, 13 March 1811

An encounter between Captain William Hoste, commanding four frigates, and a Franco-Venetian squadron under Commodore Dubourdieu, with three French frigates, three Venetian frigates and five smaller warships, off the Dalmatian coast. In a furious three-hour action the French fought in two divisions against Hoste's single, closely formed, line. Despite being outnumbered and outgunned, the British squadron drove the French flagship ashore, where it later blew up, and captured three more enemy frigates.

Amphion	32	Captain William Hoste
Cerberus	32	Captain Henry Whitby
Active	38	Captain James Gordon
Volage	22	Captain Phipps Hornby

Lake Erie, 10 September 1813

On Lake Erie, control of which was disputed during the Anglo-American War

HMS *Guerriere* (38) v USS *Constitution* (44), 19 August 1812. While cruising off the coast of Nova Scotia shortly after war had begun between Britain and the United States, Captain Isaac Hull in the *Constitution* encountered the frigate *Guerriere*, a former French ship, under Captain Richard Dacres. At about 5 pm action began in one of the war's epic ship-to-ship actions – a slugging match in which heavier American weight of shot would prevail over the British frigate's superior rate of fire. Within fifteen minutes the *Guerriere*'s mizzen mast crashed to the deck, the wreckage blocking the helm and trailing over the side, enabling the *Constitution* to assume a new position and rake her adversary for the next twenty minutes. Even as Dacres was assembling a boarding party as his last chance to rescue the situation, the main mast fell forwards, bringing down the fore mast and jib boom at the same time. Reduced to a mastless, floating wreck, the *Guerriere* struck, but so comprehensive was her shattered state that her captors deemed her fit only to be burned the next morning. (Stratford Archive)

of 1812, Captain Oliver Perry held command of two brigs, six schooners and a sloop, a force opposed by the British flotilla under Captain Robert Barclay which consisted of two ships, two brigs, one schooner and a sloop. Barclay approached the American anchorage at Put-in-Bay, whereupon Perry emerged to meet him. The American flagship was soon put out of action, but one of the brigs proceeded to break the British line and cripple three of its opponents, including Barclay's flagship. Seeing the futility of further resistance the whole British squadron had surrendered by mid-afternoon.

Detroit	19	Commander Robert Barclay
Queen Charlotte	18	Lieutenant Buchan
Lady Prevost	12	Lieutenant Bignal
General Hunter	6	--
Little Belt	3	--
Chippewa	1	--

Plattsburg, 11 September 1814

Captain George Downie, commanding the British squadron on Lake Champlain, took on the numerically equal American flotilla under Lieutenant Thomas Macdonough, who was deployed near Plattsburg. In a close-fought action lasting two hours, Macdonough's frigate, though badly damaged, outgunned Downie's flagship, which struck her flag. Deprived of necessary leadership, the British squadron thereupon followed suit.

Confiance	37	Captain George Downie Fisher
Linnet	16	Commander Daniel Pring
Chub	11	--
Finch	22	--

Plus 13 gunboats

Chronology

20 April 1792	The French Revolutionary Wars begin with the French declaration of war on Austria; Prussia joined soon thereafter, creating the War of the First Coalition
1 February 1793	France declares war on Britain, Holland and Spain, who join Austria and Prussia; Britain begins blockade of Brest and Toulon with the intention of halting the importation of food and other commodities; the Royal Navy, working in concert with the Army, begins defence of Britain's West Indian possessions and the seizure of enemy colonies
21 May 1794	Captain Horatio Nelson, with a body of sailors and marines, captures Bastia, Corsica, marking his first action in a long and distinguished career
1 June 1794	British victory over the French off Ushant, known as the 'Glorious First of June'; although 25 ships of the line commanded by Admiral Earl Howe defeat 26 French ships under Rear-Admiral Villaret-Joyeuse, a vital grain convoy from America nevertheless reaches port
January 1795	French invade and conquer the United Provinces (Holland), converting it into a satellite state known as the Batavian Republic
16 May 1795	Treaty of Basel; Prussia and Spain abandon the First Coalition and conclude peace with France
19 August 1796	Treaty of San Ildefonso; Spain allies herself with France, so imperilling the position of the British Mediterranean Fleet, which is obliged to evacuate Corsica and withdraw from the Mediterranean, apart from Gibraltar
8 October 1796	Spain declares war on Britain
14 February 1797	Admiral Sir John Jervis, despite being outnumbered by 15 to 27 ships, defeats the Spanish at the battle of St Vincent; Nelson executes a remarkable manoeuvre by engaging seven enemy ships, two of which he boards and captures in succession
11 October 1797	The British Channel Fleet, under Admiral Adam Duncan, defeats the Dutch fleet under Vice-Admiral Jan de Winter, off the north-west coast of Holland at Camperdown; Duncan captures 11 enemy ships and the Dutch commander
17 October 1797	Treaty of Campo Formio; Austria formally recognizes French annexation of the Austrian Netherlands (Belgium)
1 July 1798	General Napoleon Bonaparte lands in Egypt with an expeditionary force intended to capture Suez and threaten British control of India
1–2 August 1798	Decisive British victory over the French at the battle of the Nile in Aboukir Bay; Nelson commands a fleet for the first time, utterly overwhelming Admiral François de Brueys by doubling the French line; nine French ships are captured and two others are destroyed
29 December 1798	Russia, by allying herself with Britain, establishes the Second Coalition, to which Turkey, Naples and Portugal adhere; Austria joins in June 1799
August–October 1799	An Anglo-Russian expeditionary force fails to occupy the Batavian Republic, though the enemy fleet is captured; Russia leaves the Second Coalition as a result of failures here and in Switzerland
16 December 1800	Russia, Prussia, Denmark and Sweden form the League of Armed Neutrality as a protest against the British practice of maritime search and seizure; the existence of the League threatens Britain's access to naval supplies from the Baltic, especially timber and hemp
9 February 1801	Treaty of Lunéville; Austria concludes peace with France, which receives further territorial concessions in northern Italy
8 March 1801	A British expeditionary force lands in Aboukir Bay, beginning a campaign that will force the French to surrender Egypt five months later
2 April 1801	British naval victory at the battle of Copenhagen, where Nelson, second in command to Admiral Hyde Parker, destroys the Danish fleet while it sits anchored under the guns of the city's fortifications; in response, Russia abandons the League of Armed Neutrality
27 March 1802	Treaty of Amiens between Britain and France concludes the French Revolutionary Wars; the former restores all French and French allied colonial possessions apart from Ceylon and Trinidad; Britain pledges to evacuate Malta but refuses to do so as a result of French territorial acquisitions on the Continent

18 May 1803	Britain declares war on France; start of the Napoleonic Wars
19 October 1803	Under coercion, Spain agrees to pay a substantial subsidy to France
12 December 1804	Spain declares war on Britain
11 April 1805	Britain and Russia conclude an offensive alliance, forming the Third Coalition, to which Austria and Sweden adhere in August and November, respectively
21 October 1805	Nelson decisively defeats the Franco-Spanish fleet under Villeneuve at the battle of Trafalgar, the most decisive naval action of modern times
2 December 1805	Napoleon defeats the combined Austro-Russian army at Austerlitz in Moravia, obliging Austria to leave the Third Coalition and forcing the Russians to withdraw far to the east
6 October 1806	War of the Fourth Coalition formed, with Prussia the principal adversary against France, distantly supported by Britain and Russia; most of the latter's troops will not confront the French until February 1807
14 October 1806	Prussian forces decisively defeated by the French at the twin battles of Jena and Auerstadt; in the course of the ensuing weeks the French relentlessly pursue the remaining Prussian forces and occupy all of the principal fortresses
14 June 1807	Battle of Friedland; having already fought them to a bloody standstill at Eylau on 7 February, Napoleon decisively defeats the Russians
7–9 July 1807	Treaties of Tilsit; peace concluded between France on the one hand and Russia and Prussia on the other; Napoleon imposes a heavy indemnity on Prussia and occupies the country; Russia allies herself to France and agrees to shut her ports to British shipping; Russia declares war on Britain on 31 October
27 September 1807	Fearing that Napoleon will use Danish naval resources to re-establish the fleet lost at Trafalgar, Britain dispatches a naval and military expedition to bombard Copenhagen and seize the fleet; the Danes quickly capitulate
27 October 1807	Treaty of Fontainebleau; France and Spain conclude an alliance against Portugal
November–December 1807	French Army proceeds through Spain and occupies Portugal in an effort to close her ports to British trade
19 March 1808	King Charles IV of Spain abdicates, followed in May by his son, Ferdinand; both are imprisoned by the French, who place Joseph Bonaparte on the Spanish throne
2 May 1808	Uprising against the French in Madrid; beginning of the Peninsular War; Spain establishes a Junta and concludes peace with Britain on 4 July
1 August 1808	British expeditionary force under Sir Arthur Wellesley (later the Duke of Wellington) lands in Portugal
9 April 1809	Alliance concluded between Austria and Britain; formation of the Fifth Coalition
5–6 July 1809	Battle of Wagram; Austrians defeated in the decisive action of the campaign
14 October 1809	Treaty of Schönbrunn; Austria concludes peace with France, ceding territory in Italy and along the Adriatic
28 July 1809	Major British expeditionary force embarks for the Scheldt estuary; troops land on Walcheren Island, intending to capture Antwerp, but the outbreak of disease leads to the army's withdrawal by late December
18 June 1812	The United States, annoyed at the Admiralty's policy of naval impressment and partly motivated by territorial designs on Canada, declares war on Britain
22 June 1812	Napoleon and his Grande Armée of 600,000 men crosses the river Niemen to invade Russia
19 August 1812	USS *Constitution* (44 guns) cripples HMS *Guerriere* (38) in a half-hour engagement off Nova Scotia
10 September 1812	American naval squadron on Lake Erie crushes its British counterpart
25 October 1812	The heavy frigate USS *United States*, under the hero of the Tripolitan War, Commodore Stephen Decatur, drubs HMS *Macedonian* in a 90-minute encounter off Madeira
December 1812	Last remnants of the Grande Armée recross the Niemen after having suffered catastrophic losses during the campaign, mostly during the winter retreat
29 December 1812	USS *Constitution* wrecks the 38-gun HMS *Java* off the coast of Brazil
27 February 1813	Prussia joins Russia in forming the Sixth Coalition, together with Britain, Spain and Portugal; Sweden and Austria subsequently join, the latter on 12 August
10 September 1813	Battle of Lake Erie; Oliver Hazard Perry, commander of the American squadron, breaks the British line and annihilates Barclay's naval force
16–19 October 1813	Austrian, Russian, Prussian and Swedish forces decisively defeat Napoleon at the battle of Leipzig in Saxony; French forces, all their German allies having abandoned them, retreat to the Rhine

February–March 1814	Campaign in France; despite a number of stunning, though minor, victories Napoleon fails to stem the Allied advance on his capital
31 March 1814	Allied forces occupy Paris
6 April 1814	Napoleon abdicates and agrees to exile on the tiny Mediterranean island of Elba
19 August 1814	Admiral Sir John Cockburn's squadron disembarks British troops in Chesapeake Bay; Washington is briefly occupied and the White House burned, 24–25 August
11 September 1814	Battle of Lake Champlain; Lieutenant Thomas Macdonough, commanding the American squadron, decisively defeats his British counterpart, Captain George Downie
13 December 1814	British expeditionary force lands along the Gulf Coast near New Orleans
24 December 1814	Treaty of Ghent; peace concluded between Britain and the United States based on the status quo ante bellum; with the war over in Europe, impressment is a dead issue and does not feature in the treaty terms
1 March 1815	Sailing in secret from Elba, Napoleon lands in southern France with a small force and reaches Paris on the 20th, gathering thousands of adherents along the way; Louis XVIII abandons the capital and flees to Brussels
13 March 1815	Formation of the Seventh Coalition by Russia, Prussia, Austria and Britain
18 June 1815	The Duke of Wellington and the Prussian commander, Marshal Blücher, decisively defeat Napoleon at Waterloo, in Belgium; Napoleon abdicates on the 21st, surrenders to the British on 16 July, and is exiled to the remote south Atlantic island of St Helena, where he dies on 5 May 1821

Bibliography

The secondary literature on the Royal Navy of this period is very large. In contrast, comparatively few first-hand accounts exist of the wars and life at sea owing to the generally poor literacy of officers and the almost total inability of ordinary seamen to read or write. Those seeking information on the general workings of the Navy should consult Blake, Goodwin, Maynard and Rodger, all of which provide a basic foundation on the subject, with Lavery's *Nelson's Navy* providing even greater detail. Fighting tactics are well covered in Adkin, Davies, Gardiner, Harding, Harland, Ireland, Lambert, Tracy and Tunstall, while the battles themselves are given detailed treatment in Clowes, Ireland, Lambert, Lyon, Padfield, Rodger, Tracy and Warner. Books concentrating on Trafalgar may be easily identified from amongst the list that follows. The more technical side of the ships themselves is covered in Lavery, Davies, Gardiner, Harland, Henry and Konstam. At the opposite end of the spectrum, the Navy seen in the broad context of the age is discussed in Adkins and Adkins, Clowes, Harding, Herman, Ireland, Lambert and Padfield.

Adkin, Mark, *The Trafalgar Companion: The Complete Guide to History's Most Famous Sea Battle and the Life of Admiral Lord Nelson* London: Aurum Press, 2005

Adkins, Roy, *Trafalgar: The Biography of a Battle* London: Little Brown, 2004

Adkins, Roy, and Adkins, Lesley, *The War for All the Oceans: From Nelson at the Nile to Napoleon at Waterloo* London: Little, Brown, 2006

Ballantyne, Iain, and Eastland, Jonathan, *HMS Victory* London: Leo Cooper, 2005

Bennett, Geoffrey, *The Battle of Trafalgar* Barnsley: Wharncliffe Books, 2004

Best, Nicholas, *Trafalgar: The Untold Story of the Greatest Sea Battle in History* London: Weidenfeld & Nicolson, 2005

Blake, Nicholas, *Steering to Glory: A Day in the Life of a Ship of the Line* London: Chatham Publishing, 2005

Blake, Nicholas, and Lawrence, Richard, *The Illustrated Companion to Nelson's Navy* London: Chatham Publishing, 2005

Brownlee, Walter, *The Navy that Beat Napoleon* Cambridge: Cambridge University Press, 1980

Clayton, Tim, and Craig, Phil, *Trafalgar* London: Hodder & Stoughton Ltd., 2004

Clowes, William Laird, *The Royal Navy: A History from the Earliest Times to 1900* 7 vols. London: Chatham Publishing, 1997

Davies, David, *Fighting Ships: Ships of the Line, 1793–1815* London: Constable, 1996

Fraser, Edward, *The Sailors whom Nelson Led* London: Chatham Publishing, 2004

Fremont-Barnes, Gregory, Warrior 100: *Nelson's Sailors* Oxford: Osprey Publishing, 2005

Fremont-Barnes, Gregory, Campaign 157: *Trafalgar 1805* Oxford: Osprey Publishing, 2005

Gardiner, Robert, (ed.) *The Campaign of Trafalgar, 1803–1805* London: Chatham Publishing, 2002

Gardiner, Robert, *The Heavy Frigate: 18-pounder Frigates, 1778–1800* London: Conway Maritime Press, 1994

Gardiner, Robert, (ed.) *The Line of Battle: The Sailing Warship, 1650–1840* Annapolis, MD: Naval Institute Press, 1992

Gardiner, Robert, *Warships of the Napoleonic Wars* London: Chatham Publishing, 2003

Goodwin, Peter, *Men O'War: The Illustrated Story of Life in Nelson's Navy* London: National Maritime Museum, 2004

Goodwin, Peter, *Nelson's Victory: 101 Questions and Answers about HMS Victory, Nelson's Flagship at Trafalgar 1805* London: Brassey's, 2004

Goodwin, Peter, *The Ships of Trafalgar: The British, French and Spanish Fleets, 21 October 1805* London: Conway Maritime Press, 2005

Hall, C. D., *Wellington's Navy: Sea Power and the Peninsular War, 1807–1814* London: Chatham Publishing, 2004

Harbron, John, *Trafalgar and the Spanish Navy: The Spanish Experience of Sea Power* London: Conway Maritime Press, 2004

Harding, Richard, *Seapower and Naval Warfare, 1650–1830* London: UCL Press, 1999

Harland, John, *Seamanship in the Age of Sail* London: Conway Maritime Press, 1984

Hart, Roger, *England Expects* London: Wayland Publishers, 1972

Haythornthwaite, Philip, Elite 48: *Nelson's Navy* Oxford: Osprey Publishing, 1999

Heathcote, T. A., *Nelson's Trafalgar Captains and their Battles* Barnsley: Pen and Sword Books, 2005

Henry, Chris, New Vanguard 90: *Napoleonic Naval Armaments 1792–1815* Oxford: Osprey Publishing, 2004

Herman, Arthur, *To Rule the Waves: How the British Navy Shaped the Modern World* London: Hodder and Stoughton, 2005

Ireland, Bernard, *Naval Warfare in the Age of Sail: War at Sea, 1756–1815* New York: Norton, 2000

Konstam, Angus, New Vanguard 42: *British Napoleonic Ship-of-the-Line* Oxford: Osprey Publishing, 2001

Lambert, Andrew, *War at Sea in the Age of Sail* London: Cassell, 2000

Lavery, Brian, *The Arming and Fittings of English Ships of War, 1600–1815* London: Conway Maritime Press, 1999

Lavery, Brian, *Jack Aubrey Commands: An Historical Companion to the Naval World of Patrick O'Brian* London: Conway Maritime Press, 2003

Lavery, Brian, *Nelson's Fleet at Trafalgar* Annapolis, MD: Naval Institute Press, 2004

Lavery, Brian, *Nelson's Navy: The Ships, Men and Organisation, 1793–1815* London: Conway Maritime Press, 1992

Lavery, Brian, *Shipboard Life and Organisation, 1731–1815* London: Ashgate, 1999

Lavery, Brian, *The Ship of the Line. Vol. 1: The Development of the Battlefleet, 1650–1850* London: Conway Maritime Press, 1984

Lavery, Brian, *The Ship of the Line. Vol. 2: Design, Construction and Fitting* London: Conway Maritime Press, 1997

Lee, Christopher, *Nelson and Napoleon: The Long Haul to Trafalgar* London: Headline Book Publishing, 2005

LeFevre, Peter, *Nelson's Fleet at Trafalgar* Annapolis, MD: Naval Institute Press, 2004

Legg, Stuart, *Trafalgar: An Eyewitness Account of a Great Battle* London: Rupert Hart Davis, 1966

Lewis, Jon E., (ed.) *The Mammoth Book of Life Before the Mast* London: Robinson, 2001

Lewis, Michael A., *A Social History of the Navy, 1793–1815* London: Chatham Publishing, 2004

Lyon, David, *Sea Battles in Close-up: The Age of Nelson* Annapolis, MD: Naval Institute Press, 1996

Maine, René, *Trafalgar: Napoleon's Naval Waterloo* London: Thames and Hudson, 1957

Masefield, John, *Sea Life in Nelson's Time* Annapolis, MD: Naval Institute Press, 2002

Maynard, C., (ed.) *A Nelson Companion: A Guide to the Royal Navy of Jack Aubrey* London: Michael O'Mara Books, 2004

McGowan, Alan, *HMS Victory: Her Construction, Career and Restoration* London: Chatham Publishing, 1999

McKay, John, *100 Gun Ship "Victory"* London: Conway Maritime Press, 2000

Morriss, Roger, *The Royal Dockyards during the Revolutionary and Napoleonic Wars* Leicester: Leicester University Press, 1983

Mostert, Noel, *The Line Upon the Wind: An Intimate History of the Last and Greatest War Fought at Sea under Sail, 1793–1815* London: Jonathan Cape, 2007

Nicolson, Adam, *Men of Honour: Trafalgar and the Making of the English Hero* London: HarperCollins, 2005

Padfield, Peter, *Maritime Power and the Struggle for Freedom: Naval Campaigns that Shaped the Modern World, 1788–1851* London: John Murray, 2003

Pivka, Otto von, *Navies of the Napoleonic Era* New York: Hippocrene, 1980

Pope, Dudley, *England Expects: Nelson and the Trafalgar Campaign* London: Chatham Publishing, 1999

Pope, Dudley, *Life in Nelson's Navy* London: Chatham Publishing, 1997

Pope, Stephen, *Hornblower's Navy: Life at Sea in the Age of Nelson* London: Welcome Rain, 1998

Robson, Martin, *The Battle of Trafalgar* London: Conway Maritime Press, 2005

Rodger, N. A. M., *The Command of the Ocean: A Naval History of Britain, 1649–1815* London: Penguin, 2004

Rodger, N. A. M., *The Wooden World: An Anatomy of the Georgian Navy* London: Fontana Press, 1988

Schom. Alan, *Trafalgar: Countdown to Battle, 1803–1805* London: Penguin Books, 1992

Smith, Digby, *Navies of the Napoleonic Era* London: Schiffer Publishing, 2004

Stilwell, Alexander, (ed.) *The Trafalgar Companion* Oxford: Osprey Publishing, 2005

Terraine, John, *Trafalgar* London: Wordsworth Editions Ltd, 1998

Tracy, Nicholas, *Nelson's Battles: The Art of Victory in the Age of Sail* London: Chatham Publishing, 1996

Tunstall, Brian, *Naval Warfare in the Age of Sail: The Evolution of Fighting Tactics, 1680–1815* London: Conway Maritime Press, 2001.

Warner, Oliver, *Nelson's Battles* London: Batsford, 1965

Warner, Oliver, *Trafalgar* London: Pan Books, 1966

Winfield, Rif, *British Warships in the Age of Sail, 1793–1817* London: Chatham Publishing, 2005

Index

References to illustrations are shown
in **bold**.